to my dear friend Jean Fine

THE DYNAMICS OF COLOR

Psychological Influences

- *Personality*
- *Lifestyle*
- *Art, Music, Poetry*
- *Psychic Instinct*
- *The Chakras*
- *Meditation*
- *Consume Color*
- *Home Décor*
- *Color Healing*
- *Enlightenment*

By Polly Guerin

With Love and Admiration!

4/15/2019

Polly Guerin

Other books by Polly Guerin
. The Dollhouse Murder Mystery (Amazon 2015)
. Poetry of Reflection and Inspiration (Create Space 2015)
. The General Society of Mechanics & Tradesmen of the
  City of New York: (The History Press, Charleston. SC 2015)
. The Cooper-Hewitt Dynasty of New York (The History Press,
  Charleston, SC 2012)
. Creative Fashion Presentations Book I & II (Bloomsbury
  Publishers Inc./Fairchild Books & Visuals)
. The Stylist (Simon & Schuster Custom Publishing)
. The Story of Color (Video) Fairchild Books & Visuals

THE DYNAMICS OF COLOR

Note: The content in this book is the creative oeuvre exclusively of Polly Guerin former adjunct professor at The Fashion Institute of Technology who taught, among other subjects, color theory and color psychology.

Address inquiries to the following email: pollytalknyc@gmail.com
Visit www.pollytalk.com with direct links to Ms. Guerin's Blogs in the left-hand column on fashion, women determined to succeed, visionary men and poetry.
   Polly's weekly Blog: pollytalkfromnewyork.blogspot.com reports on New York City 's cultural and social events.

COVER ART: By David Aquino Sanchez
Soul Mates 1 Oil on Canvas

Dedicated to:

Edgar Cayce's Legendary Wisdom

and

With Loving Gratitude to Joan Baxter

TABLE OF CONTENTS

COLOR INSIGHTS FROM THE COLOR EXPERTS

The soul becomes dyed with the color or our thoughts.
                                        -Marcus Aurelius

The Story of Color is almost the story of civilization.
                                        -Faber Birren

Orange is the color of the sun. It is vital and a good color generally, indicating thoughtfulness and consideration for others.   -Edgar Cayce

I never met a color I did not like.   -Dale Chihuly

We never really perceive what color is physically.
                                        -Josef Albers

Nature always wears the colors of the spirit.
                                -Ralph Waldo Emerson

Color is a power which directly influences the soul.
                                    -Wassily Kandinsky

Green is the prime color of the world, and that from which its loveliness arises.   -Pedro Calderon de la Barca

The chief function of color should be to serve expression.
                                        -Henri Matisse

Colors, like features, follow the changes of the emotions.
                                        -Pablo Picasso

Colour in painting is like enthusiasm in life.
                                    -Vincent van Gogh

If you have to pick the wardrobe for your defense lawyer heading into court, and chose anything but blue, you deserve to lose the case.   -Carlton Wagner

"Colors express the many psychic function of man."

-Carl Jung

EDGAR CAYCE: The Most Documented Psychic of the 20th Century

Polly Guerin has had a lifelong journey exploring the theory of color psychology, which has inspired her poetry, writing, and lectures. She honed her skills by studying different holistic, metaphysical and spiritual disciplines, particularly the "readings" given on color psychology, color auras and color healing and spiritual renewal by the renowned American psychic Edgar Cayce (1877-1945). He has been called "the sleeping prophet," the "father of holistic medicine and the most documented psychic of the 20th century.

The "Readings" were the clairvoyant discourses given by Cayce while he was in a self-induced hypnotic sleep-state in which he spoke knowledgeably on a myriad of topics presented to him. At first, Cayce's psychic readings dealt mainly in physical healing, but eventually the scope of his work expanded to include advice on meditation, dreams, spiritual life, life after death, reincarnation and prophecy on world events.

Who could have known that terms such as "meditation," "spiritual growth," "auras," "soul mates," and "holistic health" would become household words to millions? In an amazing coincidence even the cover art for this book is called "Soul Mates 1."

Cayce was a humble and religious man, he never profited from his predictions, but used his reputed gift of extrasensory diagnosis, to better an individual's life purpose.

Polly's Connection: Polly has been a long time member and seminar participant, particularly on color psychology at Edgar Cayce's A.R.E., Association for Research and Enlightenment New York Center. She has also attended seminars at the Association of Research and Enlightenment, A.R.E. headquarters at Virginia Beach, VA.
Polly is a life time member of the Edgar Cayce Center of New York City and served as a Trustee, on the first Board established at the Edgar Cayce's York Center in 2012.

Her feature articles have often appeared in the New York Center's Open Door newsletter. Her latest article, SACRED SPACES, a double-page spread, appeared in the Oct-Dec, 2017 issue of the Edgar Cayce Center of New York City's OPEN DOOR newsletter, Volume XXIV, Issue 4.

As a co-founder of The Color Collective of America, with Laurie Zagon and Virginia Sullivan, Ms. Guerin worked in tandem with her colleagues and conducted seminars for the fashion industry as well as corporations, such as Fieldcrest Cannon, on the selling power of color on product production, marketing and advertising. She has also lectured extensively on how color affects mind, body and spirit, on both a personal and business level.

In addition, Ms. Guerin has penned numerous articles on the psychology of color in beauty products and lifestyle for women's interest magazines. She has also been interviewed by magazines, such as Town & Country, as well as Crain's New York Business. Then in newspaper articles, such as Newsday and Carpet Retailing, she has been referred to as a "color psychologist." Ms. Guerin's work continues to define her knowledge of the ancient wisdom of color and its modern interpretation as a mental medicine.

Author Profile

After twenty three years serving as a Professor at the Fashion Institute of Technology in New York City Ms. Guerin resigned to pursue her "brilliant writing career." At FIT she lectured extensively on the psychology of color and created the video production, THE STORY OF COLOR, produced by the publishing house Fairchild Books & Visuals, now Bloomsbury Ltd.

This video, also produced in a CD version, illustrates the language of color, the history of color identification and the influence of color psychology on fashion, home furnishings and the marketing of products. The Story of Color continues to be used today as a definitive reference in fashion and art classes. The textbooks Ms Guerin penned during her FIT tenure include Creative Fashion Presentations, Book I and II; The Stylist; Fashion Writing and another video, Creative Show Productions.

Ms. Guerin's other non-fiction books include 'The Cooper-Hewitt Dynasty of New York (The History Press, 2012) and the definitive historical book, The General Society of Mechanics & Tradesmen of the City of New York: A History (The History Press 2015). Poetry of Inspiration and Reflection and The Dollhouse Murder Mystery were also published by Amazon December 2015

LOVE OF MUSIC

Ms. Guerin's work is also greatly influenced by her love of music and early on, before discovering her writing muse, she studied to become an opera singer. She attributes the lyrical and rhythmical quality of her prose to her music training.

Currently Ms. Guerin divides her time between writing books and poetry, and contributes feature articles to Art & Antiques magazine on topics ranging from the decorative arts to antiques and collectibles. Victoriana, Art Deco, and The Little Ambassadors of Fashion are also part of her oeuvre.

The executive editor at Art & Antiques magazine once wrote: "You are one of my favorites. Not only are you prompt and professional, but your writing and reporting are top-notch. And the Art Dept. absolutely loves you."

Ms. Guerin seminars at Skidmore College, Saratoga Springs, New York included, "Writing for Magazines," as well as the "Psychology of Color in Characterization," at the (IWWG) International Women's Writing Guild conference.

Her multi-faceted career and Ms. Guerin's strong identity with color psychology makes her ideally suited to convey The *DYNAMICS OF COLOR to* her loyal readers.

"The Subject of color seems to have almost endless ramification and to touch upon life in almost every quarter, for color is rich in lore, rich in meaning and rich in purpose."

-Faber Birren

Author's Note

THE DYNAMICS OF COLOR is a book that shows you how color can whisper soft and sensuous or it can crash its way into your senses loud and clear. As such, color is an emotional experience that can touch the heart, the eyes, the taste, the sound, and the entire body with pulsating rhythms that promote good health and a positive outlook on life. Color can stimulate the imagination, the inspiration, the communication, the childlike wonder, the enchantment, the passion and the zest for life. On a broader scale certain colors can promote universal harmony and peace in the world.

Color is a common language and no matter, where you travel in the world, it is central to identifying all cultures, both ancient and modern. Color is never stagnant because each individual color in the spectrum has its own psychological message that can invoke a positive or a negative reaction.

Noted color theorist Josef Albers believed that color was a psychological phenomenon as well as an optical one. Colors, Albers said, were mood changers, and the same color could appear differently according to its surroundings.

Color can reach deep into your mind. It can be a wild, whirling experience that motivates creativity to soar to higher realms of expression. Color is so rich and complex that it can shake you, wake you, make you blink, open eyes wide, snap you to attention, set a mood and even create desire. It can also be a gentle motivator that soothes and lulls you to sleep, pacifies and calms the senses. In its most delicate stillness color can even quiet the cacophony of a computer driven environment.

Each chapter in the book discusses a specific color in the spectrum and how that color touches almost every human activity. The Dynamics of Color will help you to understand why you are drawn to a certain color. At the same time it will show how you subconsciously make color choices based on responses that are entirely your own. Individual reaction to a specific color can be based on need for fulfillment and can bring about improved health, happiness and even spiritual awakening.

This book, therefore, will help you to become aware of the healing and positive vibrations that permeate the fruit and vegetables you eat, the clothes you wear, your work and home environment, the art you patronize and even the music you listen to. Colors are multi[-faceted like people, I've never known two individuals to be exactly alike.

Thank You for Choosing

THE DYNAMICS OF COLOR

May it Enrich all the Aspects of

Your Life.

Polly Guerin

Polly

INTRODUCTION

The Dynamics of Color
and the *Rainbow*

Color has the compelling ability to touch our auditory senses in profound ways. Consider the following musical description that eludes to the spectrum's influence on music. The Spanish composer, Manuel de Falla's passionate, fast-moving zarzuela, the two-act opera, "La Vida Breve" ("The Brief Life") 1905. His first significant work, written as an entry for a competition (which it won), was described as a fiery:

"Emotional Rainbow" in which he invoked a spectrum of operatic emotions."

Sir Isaac Newton
Spectrum Colors: When Sir Isaac Newton (1672) passed a narrow stream of sunlight through a prism he identified the spectrum colors as seven colors—red, orange, yellow, green, blue, indigo and violet, which we commonly refer to as Roy GBIV.

Each color corresponds to a specific Chakra, an energy center in our body, as well as, the seven notes of the diatonic scale. Seven, therefore, is a very significant number. Just think about it; there are seven days in the week, seven openings in our head, seven seas, seven continents and many more reasons to revere the number seven.

Newton's theory of light helped to explain the origin of the rainbow from sunlight passing through raindrops that behaves like miniature prisms. That is why when we see the rainbow arc, made up of bands of spectrum colors appearing in the sky, it is caused by the refraction of the sun's rays in droplets of rain or mist. A similar arc may also be seen in a rainbow display over a waterfall or a fountain installation.

In an attempt to capture the transitory and insubstantial appearance of the rainbow, renowned painters were inspired illustrators and captured the arc in beautiful colors. This calls to mind the painting, "Home of the Rainbow, Horseshoe Falls, Niagara," by famed American landscape artist, Albert Bierstadt (1830-1902).

"Home of the Rainbow," inspired by Horseshoe Falls in Niagara, New York, is a visual experience that invites the viewer to imagine standing on the brink of the precipice, their senses engaged by the audible roar of its dynamic waters with the magnificent arc of the rainbow captured in the mist.

John Constable

In English painter, John Constable's 1827 watercolor, "Sky Study with Rainbow," he uses the medium to create an impression of intense luminescence by contrasting a series of thin arching rainbow colors against a heavily washed blue sky.

Polish-born American abstract painter, Julian Stanczak's main concern was always color, which he viewed subjectively:

"Color is abstract, universal," he said, "yet personal and private in experience. It primarily affects us emotionally, not logically, as do tangible things."

Fascination with the Rainbow

The idea that a pot of gold can be found at rainbow's end originated somewhere in Europe. Similarly, in western culture the beautiful sight of a rainbow has become a symbol of renewed hope; and the harbinger of good luck to look forward to.

Fascination with the rainbow proliferates in advertising, in logos on clothing and in songs. Alluding to hope and a happier place, The song from The Wizard of Oz, "Somewhere Over the Rainbow," which Judy Garland made famous, says it all---a rainbow can also be an illusory objective like chasing the rainbow to find happiness. For Instance, the song, "I'm ways Chasing Rainbows" seems to have taken inspiration from such a theory.

Noted color author, Ernest J. Stevens, poem, "The Rainbow," seems to sum up the rainbow in a very amusing way. "I love to paint my shutters blue, My pillars rose, my gables green, My doors a bright vermilion hue, With orange frescoes in between, And then I hear the bigwigs say, "How crude! All houses should be gray !" And then when I've tinted vacant spots of walls in some delightful tones, With gallant swirls and polka dots, And when the solemn pedants groan, "This really isn't done, you know!" I ask, "Why not? I like it so." Must all the world be dark as doom, Poor hood man-blind--- for such you be? Behold, against your timid gloom, In laughing hues of life and glee, Our radiant rainbow! Let me think; We'll make that chimney salmon-pink! "

THE DYNAMICS OF COLOR
and the Chakras

Chakras and Music: The ancient clairvoyants looked at the energy centers in the body as spinning wheels of light, color and energy, called Chakras, which in Sanskrit means "wheel."

There are seven main Chakras that resonate and vibrate to a specific color in the spectrum. Think of your body as a musical instrument. Each string (Chakra) of your musical instrument (body) actually resonates and becomes harmonized by a corresponding musical note on the C scale, (7 notes, C to G).

The Violet/White Crown Chakra, for example, (top of the head) represents enlightenment, divine wisdom and bliss. It resonates to the vocal sound "B" on the C scale. The Indigo Chakra resonates to "A," the Blue Chakra to "G," the Green Chakra to "F," the Yellow Chakra to "E," the Orange Chakra to "D" and the Red Chakra to "C" on the C Scale.

Color Instinct

It may be surprising to you to learn that you instinctively know more about color than you realize. However, this book digs deeper and demystifies the psychological aspects of color. It introduces you to simple but powerful tools to help you to effectively use the broad spectrum to improve your lifestyle, your health, your mental outlook and even your spiritual development.

The colors reflected in the spectrum have chameleon characteristics and your unique psychological responses bring about either positive or negative feelings. Those responses differ with each individual and depend upon the context in which a color is presented. Therefore, how you perceive and prefer a color is dependent on demographic factors, such as your age, ethnicity, gender and socioeconomic level. Where you live also affects your color choices. Live in the South and you tend to like strong, warm colors, whereas if you live up North, you usually prefer soft cool colors

Color choices do not remain permanent but are a daily life-changing experience. As you mature or perhaps move to another location, change your job, garner a higher standard of living, raise a family, or remarry your color choices can change as well. Color selection, therefore, is a highly individual process that has mind altering affects on your mood, your body and your spiritual outlook.

Positive/Negative

The *Dynamics of Color* explains how behavioral responses depend upon how you perceive color. Take red, for example, it relates to the sustainability of the life force itself. On the plus side red can create positive vibrations to help you to reclaim joy and vitality as your daily life-giving mantra. During his lifetime, the noted psychic, Edgar Cayce often commented about color:

"It can be a fascinating game noticing how any person with vitality and vigor will have a little splash of red in a costume, in a room, or in a garden."

While this powerful color has a commanding presence and identifies with vitality and vigor, Red also invokes instant drama. Wear Red and you evoke the persona of an extrovert; you stand out in a crowd with a "look-at-me" demand to be noticed.

We also relate to color with learned responses. Therefore red, like the other colors in the spectrum, can also represent another viewpoint. Red can be red-hot, explosive, signal danger and warn us with the sign, "do not enter."

Lighter versions of Red, called "tints," can also alter your response. The pink tint (red infused with the innocent qualities of pure white pigment) creates a softer, sweeter hue that is associated with a romantic, more durable love, while vibrant red is fiery and passionate.

Case in point, Swiss born artist, Ferdinand Hodler, of the early twentieth century, attributed symbolic meaning to the colors in his paintings and associated red with passion.

COLOR in ARCHITECTURE Why do men and women develop nervous conditions, even depression in gray buildings? Its lack of color in our architecture that produces that tired feeling. Business sections of cities need to punctuate their buildings with color to psychologically provide more uplifting reaction to interior surroundings and particularly the building's exterior. Perhaps something about this has caught on because recently in addition to the Empire State Building, many other buildings are lighting up at night with colorful displays to project a specific identity with their edifice. Case in point, a sports arena chose a dominant RED lighting theme to attract pedestrian's to its center of high energetic activity.

The Dynamics of Color
Defining Color

It is not easy to define color because it is a non-verbal communicator, a message of beauty that is in the eye of the beholder, a figment of an individual's imagination. To the physicist, however, color is determined by the wavelength of light. It is only when electromagnetic light waves of particular lengths interact with the cone cells in the retina that your brain "sees" colors.

RED Vibrations

Red, for example, has the longest wavelength and registers a strong visual, attention-grabbing impact. That is why red is the dominant color in the commercial world in product labeling, merchandise assortments, advertising. It says 'Buy Me.'
Red is also a motivating color and identifies with fast food restaurants that want you to eat fast and move out of the restaurant in record time to make room for other people eager to dine and dash.

YELLOW Visibility

On a scale of high visibility bright yellow, sometimes called neon yellow, and bright orange are two colors that stand out as the colors of choice for utility uniforms and vehicles because these colors can readily be seen from a distance.

PRIMARY Colors

Red, Blue and Yellow are pure primary colors and cannot be made by using any combination of other colors. Instead, the primaries are the kingpins responsible for making the secondary and tertiary colors.

SECONDARY Colors

The secondary colors are a combination of two primary colors. They are orange (a combination of red and yellow), green (blue and yellow) and purple (blue and red). Variations of the secondary colors will produce lighter tint versions. For example, lavender is a tint, a derivative of purple.

TERTIARY Colors

The tertiary colors are a combination of a primary and a secondary color. The color name becomes hyphenated. For example, yellow with green becomes yellow-green and in the fashion world it is often called Chartreuse.

In literature writers take poetic license and refer to color and the spectrum with interesting dialogue. One such example is found in the book , *"Brideshead Revisited" by Evelyn Waugh.*

After dinner when Anthony and the narrator Charles Ryder drink Chartreuse Anthony muses, "There is a fine distinct taste as it trickles over the tongue. It's like swallowing a spectrum."

WHITE & BLACK

White has its own identity outside of the color spectrum. It reflects sunlight and therefore embodies all the seven colors in the spectrum. White motivates kindness, it evokes a quiet independence and a peace-loving nature.

Black is also an outsider and lacking light emitting qualities, it represents the absence of color. Too much focus on black can result in various forms of gloom or depression. Yet, on a positive note, it can make a strong statement as a chic and glamorous color, especially in fashion and home décor.

THE DYNAMICS OF COLOR
Storytelling

COLOR ORIGINS: The birth of the rainbow is steeped in legends, folklore and many ancient legends. In Greek mythology, Iris was the goddess of the rainbow, a bridge between Heaven and earth, and the messenger of the gods.

In ancient legends Australian aborigines believed that the birth of the fiery Opal gemstone is traced to when the creator came down to Earth on a rainbow in order to bring the message of peace to all humans. Then at the very spot, when his foot touched the ground, the Opal stone became alive and started to sparkle in all the colors of the rainbow.

Opal's chameleon rainbow colors are said to reflect people's changing emotions and moods, and for ages people believed in the healing power of Opal to solve depression. On a positive note, it was thought that the opal would help them find true, romantic love.

Color is also affected by culture and certain colors can mean something entirely different in another country. White for brides in America and Red for Brides in Japan. This book, however, addresses the psychology of color as it is understood in the West.

The Dynamics of Color identifies each color's personality traits, qualities and functions. The book demystifies the psychological effects of color with historical facts, a color's Chakra relationship, its musical association and aroma sensitivity. In addition, the author describes each color's influence on fashion, home furnishings and products. She also describes how the colorful variety of food we eat strongly relates to life-saving benefits and a healthy outcome.

FOOD and COLOR

It is interesting to note that in a similar take on food and color, the artist Tattfoo Tan developed the Nature Matching System (NMS) as a reminder to us to daily consume our recommended ingestion of color.

Tattfoo said "The intense colors of every fruit and vegetable are nature's nutrition labels. They get many of their colors from phytonutrients, compounds that play key roles in health and help to reduce the risk of heart disease and cancer. The more colors that come together in a meal, the better."

Tattfoo Tan's huge street-wide, panoramic mural installation, 'Remember to Take Your Daily Dose of Color,' caused a sensation and reminded passersby as the palette of produce matched each color with its food source. It was exhibited at the Port Authority Bus Terminal in New York City in 2008. In describing his installation Tattfoo Tan said, "It is truly a rainbow connection." Later Tattfoo Tan's installation moved on to other cities in the United States.

TRIVIA and COLOR

The "Trivia" section of the book is both interesting and informative, sometimes amusing. It may remind you about anecdotes and sayings and that you already know or have heard over the years, but it also provides interesting phrases and familiar words to add to your color vocabulary.

You may not realize it, but you are color personified, and your physical body consists of all the colors in the spectrum, red blood, blue veins for example. Most people often identify with a specific color, but on any given day your physical need or mood may change. One day, you could feel the need for blue for serenity, another day red for energy or green for balance. The color choice you make depends on the day, the circumstances and the state of your emotional conditioning.

CHAMELEON COLOR

Color therefore is a life-changing agent. Since it strongly affects your physical well being or mood, it is important to understand the psychology of color. Selecting the wrong color can make you feel agitated, discomforted or discouraged.

The Dynamics of Color goes beyond the surface of color erudition. It takes you on a comprehensive color journey of enlightenment. This self-help book, therefore, is both informational and inspirational. As your own personal guide it will help you to make better, more effective color choices from which you will garner life-changing benefits.

A poem inspired by color psychology introduces each chapter. Written by the author in captivating verse, each poem reveals the unique psychological qualities that relate to a specific primary (red, blue, yellow), secondary (green, orange, purple), achromatic (black, white, gray), tertiary colors, neutrals or pastels (pink, baby blue, pale yellow).

I hope that you will have great pleasure and many occasions to re-read and enjoy *The Dynamics of Color*. Congratulations!!! You have wisely chosen the wisdom of color psychology to jump start your journey on the colorful path to personal happiness, success and enlightenment.

Polly Guerin
Author/Poet

The Dynamics of Color
Legends and Folklore

"The story of color is almost the story of civilization itself,"said the famed color authority and scientist, Faber Birren. "All nature was colored and ancient man tried to emulate it. Color was identified with the sun, the stars, the rainbow, and looked upon with wonder and awe."

Ancient civilizations of Atlantis, Lemuria, Nu and Alatia used color in therapeutic practices. So did the Egyptians, who were world's ahead of the New Age thinkers. Legend has it that this enlightened society built temples where color healing took place. Sunlight was projected through colored gems, such as rubies and sapphires, onto people seeking healing.

They also used pulverized gemstones in remedies for sickness--yellow beryl, for example, as a cure for jaundice. Just as women today covet the secrets of beauty and a youthful appearance when Egyptian women were seeking rejuvenation they entered The Temple Beautiful to bask in different colors for healing or rejuvenation. (Gimbel, Healing With Color and Light, p. 21)

Doesn't this Egyptian wisdom remind you of the practitioners today who similarly use gemstones as a talisman to treat or improve health? Indeed, gem stone therapy has become very popular today by people seeking non-evasive alternative treatments to improve mind, body and spirit.

In ancient times color was a language. Every hue had definite significance. What early man chose for his garments, artifacts, or temples had less to do with modern conceptions of aesthetics than with a sort of occult functionalism. The very mysteries of life prescribed his palettes and he expected colors to protect him on earth, guide him safely to heaven, and symbolize the majesty of the universe. (Birren, p. 12-13.)

Nearly every race and civilization has had definite ideas about color. Native American Indians had colors designated for a nether world, as generally black, and an upper world of many colors. Red, yellow and black were considered masculine colors; white, blue, green are feminine. (Birren, p. 15)

Across the world in Tibet, the very moods of human beings have a mystical relationship to color. Light blue is celestial. Gods are white, goblins red, devils black. Similarly even in modern times, color continues to affect person's mood on either a positive or negative level. Furthermore, the ancient theory about the meaning of color has not changed: blue for sky, white for God, black for the devil. (Birren, p. 15)

Sanskrit teachings from Tibet well over 2000 years ago talk about "Chakras" energy centers in the body. There are seven Chakras that correspond to the seven colors that lie in line with the spine. (Gimbel p. 64)

The entire Chakra system acts like a prism, which corresponds to the spectrum as follows:

Violet and the White Light Chakra (the crown) is the center of creative visualization and connects you to an infinite intelligence.

Indigo Chakra (the brow) is the spiritual "Third Eye" and promotes intuitive thinking and a higher lever of consciousness.

The Blue Chakra (the throat, nose, ears, and mouth) is the center for creative expression and fosters the ability to communicate. In health matters blue battles throat ailments including laryngitis.

The Green Chakra (the heart) is the color of balance and the center of harmony, understanding, compassion and unconditional love.

The Yellow Chakra (the solar plexus) symbolically relates to the stomach and digestion. Like the sun it descends into the nervous system and is the center of happy feelings.

The earthier, Orange Chakra, (the spleen) rules the lower intestines, kidneys and adrenal glands. Orange promotes vitality and makes you feel youthful.

At the base of the spine, is the Red Chakra, (the root). It is the center of sexuality connected to passion, the life force itself, energy and the power to create. (Gimbel, p.64-65)

According to Chakra practitioners the Chakra colors can be used to improve one's health or state of mind. For example, when you have a sore throat the Blue Chakra (the throat) is out of balance. Tying a blue scarf around your neck will help to soothe a sore throat or improve communication.
(Guerin, Healing With Color)

If your love life is lagging the color Red in the bedroom décor can put passion back into romance and a white ceiling can signify pure bliss.

To the ancient Buddhists of India, man himself was a product of colors and the elements: the yellowness of earth, the blackness of water, the redness of fire, the greenness of wood and the whiteness of metal. (Birren, p. 18)

The Chinese have always diagnosed illness by reading the"color" of pulses, complexion, and the appearance of the body's tissues and organs. A red pulse indicates a numbness of heart, whereas a yellow pulse means the stomach is healthy.
(Gimbel, p. 21)

No wonder, when we visit a Chinese doctor today one of the first things they might do is to check our pulse, or look at the tongue or nails to ascertain one's condition of positive or negative health.

In Europe the science of Heraldry had its medieval roots in color symbolism. During the crusades the English soldier wore a white cross, the Frenchman a red cross and the Fleming a green one. Heraldry remains part of modern culture, particularly in England. (Birren, p. 48)

Color was also vital to the doctrine of the Four Humours. The Greek physician, Hippocrates (460-510 BC) developed a medical theory that was common throughout Europe from the days of the ancient Greeks and Romans to the Renaissance. Each humour was assigned its own color and any imbalance in the humours was manifested in the color of the skin complexion, tongue, urine, and feces. (Gimbel, p. 21)

Liturgical stained glass windows in cathedrals and churches throughout the world are a perfect example of how the ancestors relied upon daylight to illuminate the spiritual symbolism of color for meditation and prayer. The French stained glass artisan family, Maumejean Freres, a prolific producer of liturgical windows, received the grand prix at the 1925 Paris Exposition Internationale des Arts Industriels Modernes for their exquisite window,"The Annunciation." It is a stunning interpretation of glass caught in a web of leaded metal: red symbolized the life force, blue represented the celestial, the godly sphere and gold exalted the rays of wisdom through the illumination of the sun. (Guerin, Stain Glass Tapestries)

Color is an important part of culture. The scared and profane holidays of a modern world bear tribute to the convenience, if not the divinity of the spectrum in glorifying things festive. Red belongs to Christmas, St. Valentine's Day and the Fourth of July. Green is for St. Patrick's Day. Yellow and purple are for Easter, and orange for Thanksgiving and Halloween.

Flowers also have symbolic meaning. A charming custom, in celebration of Spring, the first of May's flower is the Muguet, the white Lily of the Valley. Wearing the white carnation on Mother's day is for the deceased, while the red carnation is for the living. (Birren, p. 50)

Chapter I
THE DYNAMICS OF COLOR
Color Psychology

WHITE
Purity and Innocence

Soft, inviting fresh air clean
Dazzling white is so supreme

Think of pristine driven snow
Vanilla ice cream that we know

Cool for summer fashion wear
Lighthearted mood without care

Purity of spirit and angelic ways
Brides' choice, innocent praise

On wavelengths of originality
White evokes clear practicality

White is pure divine perfection
Like a frothy cake confection

Radiates all colors, powerful way
White is rich and supreme all day

Clear visions of clouds in the sky
Spiritually rich don't question why

Just know that white's sentiment
Clears the path to enlightenment

Chapter I
THE DYNAMICS OF COLOR
Color Psychology

WHITE
Purity and Innocence

White resonates with thoughts of heavenly bliss. It is so pure, so innocent, so youthful, so revered for its high status in fashion, sports and the medical profession. When Isaac Newton (1642-1727) guided a shaft of sunlight through a glass prism in a darkened room white light separated into its seven constituent colors---the colors of the spectrum: red, orange, yellow, green, blue, indigo and violet. Put simply, white contains all the colors of the spectrum and therefore has all the qualities of the colors within its orbit. (Guerin/The Story of Color)

White speaks volumes: Peace on earth, delicacy, pearls, porcelain, pristine snow, angels, swans, fluffy clouds, popcorn, rice, coconut, ivory, lace, chalk, the moon.

The spiritual aspects of white are legendary. To believers, white prayers release pure results and white thoughts clear the path to heavenly aspirations. White, associated with prayer and spirituality, brings an individual, it is said, to a higher plane and closeness to God. As White conjures up the purity of spirit and the angelic qualities of innocence it releases a new sense of freedom on wavelengths of originality.

It is no wonder, therefore, that certain religious groups wear white to symbolize purity of heart and a desire for simplicity. However, when white is worn for reasons other than religious convictions, it may suggest someone who may be rather immature, a person who wishes to retreat from the realities of everyday life.

White has universal appeal. With all the positive vibrations of the spectrum colors in its orbit white may be your first choice for spiritual renewal. Think guardian angels that legends say protect and guide us in our daily life.

A white personality is often described being perfectly pure of mind and spirit. White also reminds us of innocence, virginity and youthfulness. A person so imbued can be bashful and demure with child-like wonder.

The power of the mind is amazing. Like the ancient Egyptians, modern seekers also meditate on the Chakras, the energy centers in our body, to activate positive fulfillment of a spiritual nature.

The VIOLET and WHITE LIGHT CHAKRA, (the crown) for example, located at the top of your head, brings you into the orbit of divine thoughts, godliness, spiritual enlightenment and pure love. The Violet and White Light Chakra represents high intelligence, and is the origin of creativity, purity of thoughts and aspirations.

The Violet ray brings you closer to divine realization, humility and stimulates creative imagination. It is said that a true devotee of violet, through meditation, can create their heart's desire. The violet ray has a soothing and tranquilizing effect. The nineteenth-century chromotherapist Edwin D. Babbitt viewed violet as capable of cooling nerves.
(The Color Compendium, p. 310)

Creative individuals may particularly benefit from a dose of violet, particularly artists, actors and musicians who by their nature tend to be high strung. Like these artistic types, whenever anxiety overcomes your efforts to concentrate, focus on violet for creative fulfillment and productivity.

VISUALIZATION: You probably don't realize it, but you inherently possess a beautiful spark of white light that can be engaged to use in a visualization technique to clean and clear negativity and restore peace and confidence. *Edgar Cayce, the great American prophet, encouraged the positive potentials of visualization, because the spiritual aspects of white brings you to a higher plane and closeness to God.*

Advertisers also know something about visualization and continually play with our minds. They tell us: "Picture Yourself in a brand-new Mercedes..." or "Picture Yourself looking out from the balcony of your oceanfront Hawaiian condo." So, if advertising can help us to visualize, it is quite simple to therefore target your own personal needs to improve mind, body and spirit. Simply put the power of your mind into focus to actualize a specific change you want to make or to fulfill your heart's desire.

VISUALIZATION, however, requires a great deal of self-discipline, concentration and focus. It suggests that you totally immerse yourself in the White Light of Spirit, which symbolizes the sum total of all the spectrum colors. It is a visualization practice that claims to cleanse the debris, the toxic waste out of one's system.

In simple terms, imagine the presence of a glowing white light at the top of your head beaming brightly and radiating down through your body with rays of wisdom.

Then very, very, very slowly as you visualize yourself sending the white light throughout your entire body, very gently let it penetrate every limb. At the same time as you are doing this technique repeat, yes repeat, the affirmation: "I am cleansing my body of negativity and purifying my mind, body and spirit." Or you may have a specific healing need and can change the affirmation to accommodate the desire for a personal outcome..

It is essential to do this technique in a quiet environment where you can concentrate and be totally undisturbed. Never expect immediate results. You may need to patiently practice the visualization technique over several days, maybe weeks. Remember that visualization is not a shortcut--it simply assists you to reach your goal. The most satisfying result is the complete peace that you will feel after a visualization exercise.

MUSIC: Did you ever wonder why certain notes in the musical scale heighten your sensitivity and you begin to see a specific color? That is because every Chakra is in tune with a specific color in the spectrum and music's healing vibrations affect your health and well being.

Hal A. Lingerman in the book, "The Healing Energies of Music" said, "I believe great music, carefully selected and experienced, is a unique agent for healing, attunement, inspiration and expanded spiritual consciousness."

Throughout history musicians have seen color in relationship to music. Father Castel, in 1763, created a color music scale that could flash colored lights in time to musical notes.

Other inspired musicians have also tried to identify color and music, but the color-music reference in this book relates to the C scale. Violet, for example, resonates to the musical note "B" and the vowel sound, "Ohm."

Creative individuals might take a color cue from German composer, Richard Wagner (1813-83) who is considered one of the most influential composers of all time, notably his Ring cycle and his last great work, Parsifal. It is said that he placed violet curtains in front of himself when he desired to compose high, spiritual music. While great works of music may energize and inspire some of the new age music with discordant tones may irritate or depress. Therefore it is important to chose music wisely, not only for yourself, but especially for young people who may become influenced by negative vibes. Today the choice of music to heal and inspire proliferates. Consider your need, be it spiritual or merely to soothe frazzled nerves or combat stress; there's something special in music for everyone.

THE ART WORLD

John Singer sergeant played a critical role in choosing what attire his sitters wore in his paintings. He chose simplicity, shimmering white ballgowns for his 1899 portrait of the Wyndham Sisters, Lady Elcho, Mrs. Adeane and Mrs. Tennant. This intimate trio setting reflects the regal elegance of white in synergistic ostentation.

The purity of white also calls to mind the pristine sculpture, Bird in Space, (1923) by Constantin Brancusi. Its white slender projectile is a mesmerizing testament to the power of white.

FASHION IMPACT

The French couture House of Worth knew the dramatic impact of white would convey the right message of innocence in a fashionable 1890s white wedding gown created by Charles Frederick Worth. Now housed at the Metropolitan Museum of Art's Costume Collection the white gown with its dramatic hourglass silhouette and enormous gigot sleeves suggests the virginal purity of the wearer's character.

A Fashionable Impression: Wear white if you want to project an image of refined elegance and impeccable grooming. White is a high status color that suggests wealth and leisure, someone who can afford expensive cleaning bills. When an image of authenticity is desired white is the logical choice. It says that high on the list of your priorities is honesty, integrity and faithfulness.

White is a summer essential. Think of terms like "tennis whites"and you visualize crisp, cool sports outfits. Summer white fashions like a pristine white city costume reflects heat and keeps you cool and comfortable. The 'Spectator Look,' a white suit worn with brown and white wing-tip ladies shoes and a matching handbag says you're classic and ready for a job interview. White is the perfect foil for bright accessories.

Think of the dramatic contrast of a white outfit worn with a lipstick red bead necklace and matching red patent handbag. The clash of red with white says you're an extrovert. A white jacket worn with another color in the spectrum, such as, a cobalt blue skirt accessorized with a matching multi-colored scarf conveys a lively and well-balanced personality. You can create a stunning twenty-four carat look by coordinating a white outfit with gold leather accessories: a handbag, matching belt, shoes, and headband. It conveys a stunning image and says you're a golden girl, rich and high-minded.

Fashion's doyenne of draping, French designer Madame Alix Gres sculpted pleated white silk jersey into an evening gown reminiscent of a Classical Greek artifact, and turned women into living statues. Such a sculpted gown says you are regal, austere and at the height of sophistication.

White lends a powerful image to the classic Chanel suit created by celebrated Parisian couture designer, Gabrielle "Coco" Chanel. Stunning with Chanel's military-influenced boxy jacket, is the quintessential accessory a white camellia on a black satin ribbon, which can be worn tied at the neck or worn as a hair ornament. It says that you are couture fashionista and self-assured about your fashion image.

Evening wear fashions saturated in white offer dressy modern possibilities. A white lace bustier sprinkled with faux diamonds and worn with white stretch skintight cigarette pants says you're strong- minded, confident and determined to make heads turn. A long white silk strapless gown, finely pleated in the Grecian Goddess style inaugurated by Madame Gres is still a stunning chic look. On a well-tanned woman it is the ultimate vision of sophistication.

TEXTILES: However, textiles tell a different story. The innocence of white lends itself to textural patterns like eyelet, embroidery and embossed embellishments. Especially pretty in summer dresses texture is preferred by the "jeune filles set" (young girls). They like openwork and texture to add surface intrigue to their outfits.

On the more mature side, a fashionable woman dressed in a white costume of a rigid texture, like gabardine, suggests a certain degree of sophistication and savoir-faire. Wearing white, head to toe drama, portrays a certain class of society, evoking an aristocratic impression. It says you are a fashionista who is cool and chic.

In contrast, however, seemingly weightless white tulle, voile or sheer cotton batiste may connote a woman that is fragile and dainty. Floating on the air of innocence and naivete she symbolically portrays the ingenue, the invalid, the daydreamer, the fairy princess.

However, if your aim is to jump start creativity, wearing violet, a complement to white, can enrich your imagination and ideas flow freely. Spiritually minded women chose white for inspiration and artistic women often chose violet as do people who create crafts for a living. A pastel lilac scarf or shawl added to a white outfit is the perfect look for a woman who wants to enhance her artistic and spiritual potential.

LACE: Few fabrics convey as much meaning as White Lace. Like the icing on a wedding cake lace evokes fond memories of innocence and purity: a baby's christening gown, a traditional wedding dress, the lace headpiece or shawl a woman wears to church, and the Jewish matriarch who defines her role in Sabbath celebrations wearing a lace head covering. Harking back to grandmother's time think about the white heirloom lace tablecloth laid out for the holidays. Then there's the role of white lace in boudoir lingerie. Nothing could be more enticing or bridal.

Virginal White: "The Bride Wore Red," the title of a feature story I wrote for "Doll World" magazine, records that up to the Victorian era wedding gowns were not angelic white. Women merely wore their best Sunday attire. It was not uncommon therefore, for a bride to wear a red gown.

In the nineteenth century the popularity of the a lace embellished white gown with flowing veil, as we know it today, is credited to Queen Victoria who started the tradition when she married Prince Albert in 1840. Queen Victoria commemorated her marriage with the following diary entry: "I wore a white satin gown with a deep flounce of Honiton lace, imitation of old. I wore my Turkish diamond necklace and earrings, and Albert's beautiful sapphire brooch."

Even today, when a bride is not necessarily a virgin, she still wears white on the theory that it symbolically cancels out her previous experiences so that she enters the marriage with pure thoughts and innocent expectations.

On the more spiritual side of the palette wearing white signifies purity of heart, religious intentions and an urge for the simpler things in life. In hospitals white uniforms and white interiors convey an image of cleanliness and professionalism, and to the believer the spiritual aspects of white brings one closer to recovery and restoration of health.

HOME FURNISHINGS: You may love the drama of an entirely white decorating scheme, but remember white requires high maintenance to maintain its pristine clean appearance. A white leather sofa or plush white carpeting suggests a household that can not only indulge in luxurious purchases, but it also says they can afford to be extravagant and somewhat impractical. Nonetheless, if white is your choice, it is best spiced up with primary or secondary colors for a more balanced ambiance.

On a positive note, the pure color association of white with spiritual enlightenment makes it an ideally choice for room décor where meditation is the focus.

White wicker furniture has a different, more romantic story. On the porch or sun room white wicker reminds us of Victorian refinement and those halcyon summer days sipping lemonade on the wrap-around porch. A wicker bedroom ensemble: dressing table, bed and chairs are a refreshing addition to a young girl's bedroom and looks pretty with white eyelet or red and white gingham bed and pillow accessories.

White may be a heavenly color, but here on earth white has the natural ability to act like a psychological air conditioner. Its stark appearance can seemingly cool down a room that is located in a hot zone in the house or apartment. That is why when some individuals are immersed in such a sterile white environment they psychologically claim to feel cold. If this is the case, then a tonic of color from the warm side of the spectrum like red, yellow or orange, worked into the environment will change that impression.

White is both emotional and visually exciting. Although white in home decor may connote spanking clean cleanliness and minimalism, with time, its bland no-nonsense persona can become boring. To counterbalance this negative effect white furnishing can be made to look more inviting when a healthy balance is established by using warm colors plucked from the rainbow: red, yellow or orange, in decorative toss pillows, throws or lampshades. A white room can also take on a dramatic venue. Just add one big bold piece of furniture like a bright lipstick red recliner and it conveys an eye-popping impression.

ALTERING SPACE: Color can alter space, make it appear smaller or larger. With space at premium for most small-scale apartments, a low ceiling room can be made to appear seemingly higher when you paint the ceiling white and the walls a happy color. Decorator touches require just a little bit of imagination. If you're an environmentalist, invite the outdoors into your home. Consider painting a white picket fence around the wall in a child's playroom, and then add a background to simulate a park playground. Then too, painting white clouds on a blue ceiling can create a celestial mood room. Violet is an excellent color in areas of the house where creativity is an essential part of work or play. It aids in the development of one's imagination and encourages inspiration.

PRODUCTS that evoke the image of cleanliness or purity do so through the use of white packaging or bottle labeling. "Think white and it conjures up fluffy-towels and a breath of fresh laundry," so says a new just-laundered new scent collection.

White detergents appear powerful and effective. Just walk down the aisle with white packaged household cleaning products. They suggest sterility and cleanliness. Firms that want to tell customers, that they part of the green movement and are environmentally concerned, have adapted white and green labeling on packaging.

When white is the dominant in the sell of diet products it conveys the message that the product has lightweight qualities and less calories. Think yogurt, low fat cottage cheese, and 1% or 2% milk.

The wrong color can really hurt sales. An attempt was made to produce the popular beverage, Coca-Cola, in a white version. However, because of traditional taste, the white beverage did not find overwhelming acceptance.

However, the beauty industry tempts the consumer to purchase products that clarify, purify and restore one's beauty. However, you would rarely see a white foundation, but there are exceptions. A major cosmetic firm offers "Beyond Natural," a weightless foundation that goes on white and then self-adjusts to match your natural skin tone so you can look naturally glamorous. And another white foundation powder with the essence of white pearl has the promise of a glowing complexion.

Then too, there's a women's scent called, "Love in White," which has a softer, powdery and more girly scent that evokes the message of youthful ingenuity.

The relationship of color to products has permeated other areas of feminine appeal. The science of perfume, for example, includes fragrances, in which the ingredients called; "notes" are tuned into a specific color in aromas such as lotus, rose and olibanum.

EAT YOUR COLOR: In the abundant market selection of vegetables and fruits different colors provide significant health benefits. Therefore, a healthy diet should include a spectrum of colors in your daily menu. When adding white to the mix, think mushrooms, tofu, cauliflower, white endive and coat cheese-- these all suggest less calories. Low fat milk provides calcium for good bones and teeth as does low fat cottage cheese. Another Low fat plus is yogurt, but check the label for products that contain probiotics, the beneficial bacteria that stimulates your energy.

Want to lose weight? A recent study found that yogurt containing L.casei (listed in the ingredients), can speed the breakdown of fat molecules helping you to shed pounds faster. A daily dosage of garlic, which contains allyl sulfides, is a good thing, too, because it can help to stop bad cells (cancer cells) from growing, so say medical practitioners.

Resent research also shows that onions, which resemble the body's cells, actually help clear waste materials from all of the cells. Onions usually produce tears, which wash the epithelial layers of the eyes.

Have you been eating your coleslaw? A nutritionist, at the American Institute for Cancer research explains that eating coleslaw is linked with a reduced risk of a number of cancers. Isothiocyanate, a phytonutrient that's abundant in coleslaw's main ingredient helps to stop cancer cells from forming, especially those that affect the breasts, lungs, stomach and colon.

TRIVIA: Word associations with white have symbolic meaning. A White Knight take over in the corporate world suggests a positive change in management. However, the White Knight in religion symbolizes Saint Michael who slays the dragon of modern personal problems. Perfumer Lalique's White Knight is called "White," a new fresh fragrance for men.

Imagine the startling impact of THE WHITE CITY, aka the Columbian Exposition,(1893), which commemorated the 400th anniversary of the discovery of America by Columbus. It became known as The White City because of the white exterior of the major exposition buildings. When illuminated at night, it was a spectacular display,which ushered in the age of electricity.

Then there's the Great White Fleet of 16 newly painted WHITE battleships which were sent in 1906-08 on a good will world peace tour by Theodore Roosevelt (Teddy, "T.R." the 26th president of the United States (1901-09). Imagine if you will visualize the impact and the impression White conveyed to emphasize the peaceful intent of the tour.

Again n 1908 the Great White Fleet, then off the coast of Egypt, was sent by President Roosevelt to help in the recovery and rebuilding of Italy, after a massive earthquake that killed up to 200,000 people. This was one of the first and greatest acts of humanitarian assistance this country has performed for a foreign country.

White pearls are a wish waiting to come true. If you were born in June, your birthstone is Pearl. Wearing white pearls have a calming affect and convey a persona of sophistication and elegance. Just remember how Michelle Obama's sheath dress and power pearls made headlines.

A fashion guru advises, "Don't just accessorize with classic pearls pile it on with multiple strands or intertwined ropes."

However, women born in April can lay claim to flawless, brilliant Diamonds as their birthstone. Diamonds are indeed a girl's best friend. This gem is touted to improve your power of pondering or concentration, which will surely help you to activate the fulfillment of your heart's desire and receive the anticipated diamond engagement ring. However, we don't want to receive a White Elephant wedding gift, something that 's a 'hard-to-get-rid of item.'

When it comes to healing, the power of diamonds is legendary. Known as the hardest of stones it was touted to cure everything, especially to fortify the mind and body.

The White Camellia has a special place in history. It was the favorite flower of Violetta, the tragic courtesan in Giuseppe Verdi's opera, La Traviata, which was based on Alexander Dumas' play, La dame aux Camellias (1852) with libretto by Francesco Maria Piave (1853).

The fragrant white blossom became symbolic with the chic little black dress. Famed Paris Couturier, Gabrielle (Coco) Chanel (1883-1971) claimed the white camellia as her own and it famously decorated the classic Chanel suit. It also became a popular hair and neck wear accessory.

When it comes to telling fibs there's the little White Lie, something minor that is forgivable. Then, too, there's Lily White which connotes goodness and purity and Little White Prayers seemingly forgive sin and restore virtue and innocence. However, White Fang, symbolic of a brave beast of epic proportions, has storybook significance.

White Rage, in a stressed society, relates to emotions that are stirred up by fear. We listen to White Noise, an indescribable sound, from a machine that seemingly blots out noise and helps us to go to sleep. Then just in time for Thanksgiving there are ghost pumpkins, so called because their outer skin is cloudy white instead of orange.

Without exaggerating we all need White in our lives because it contains all the positive qualities of each individual ray in the rainbow. White is sensitive and serene. It moves and transforms us with a feeling of purification and oneness with the universe.

VIOLET, a color component of the Crown Chakra, has loftier values to soothe stress and uplift one's spirit. Take a bath in "Violet," a natural wellness product or scrub yourself with triple milled lavender soap from Provence, France and you'll be lulled into a sense of heightened inspiration. Wear a semi-precious violet stone and sharpen your intuition and jump start creativity. Sleep on lilac scented pillows to dream up bright ideas.

Then, too, why not spray a lavender scent to ban odors from a room . Turn to nature and let the pungent aroma of lilac flowers waft through the air to remind us to stop and retreat from the demands of life. Instead luxuriate in the silence, take time to tune into your muse.

Amethyst, clear quartz and Alexandrite also relate to the Crown Chakra, which conveys the message that you are in total harmony and both mentally and spiritually attuned to an awareness of higher consciousness.

White and violet bring to the seeker the benefits of both purity and creative inspiration. Although white is devoid of any distinctive hue, it embodies all the colors in the spectrum in its luminous ray. The term, violet, is derived from a plant or flower, but by any other name it would not be as uplifting or would it be as inspirational.

Need a break? Do nothing for at least fifteen minutes and simply experience a few moments into the silence of pure white serenity or dwell on violet to connect with your creative muse.

THE DYNAMICS OF COLOR
Color Psychology

INDIGO/PURPLE
Artistic Wisdom

Purple contains the best of both--
The cool of blue, the warmth of red

The blue soul of power it is imbued
Vigorous Red persistence is renewed

Art, music and poetry take bloom
Divine ideas noble thoughts assume

The color of the great orator
Can be verbose, an intimidator

A remarkable mind, abiding wisdom
Finely tuned senses in the system

The color of mourning so victorious
The imperial color was notorious

Sanctioned for a royal entourage
Bolder, more passionate at large

Pomposity, elegance in all its glory
The fashion for purple, another story

Think eggplant, plum, orchids, too
This noble hue halts stress, renews

Purifies thoughts and emotions
Clears away despondent notions

True peacemakers and humanitarians
Unselfish workers and egalitarian

Purple's transmutation has appeal
Uplifts vibrations to high ideals.

Chapter 2
THE DYNAMICS OF COLOR
Color Psychology

INDIGO/PURPLE
Artistic Wisdom

High-minded individuals visualize Indigo to sharpen their intuition and to acquire wisdom along their path of enlightenment. The Indigo ray is a deep dark blue color, a velvety shade that embraces deep blue with warm red, and is associated with the spiritual eye of the Indigo Chakra (the brow).

Indigo opens the mind to the highest attainment of spiritual awareness and fosters the imaginative powers of devotion, intuition and creativity. Such a person is inspired by their artistic sensibilities and their out-of-the-box initiatives. Abundant ideas seem to flow effortlessly, one right after the other.

Indigo people are also the nonconformists, the innovators. They count among their orbit the super stars, the movie and theatrical performers. There is no one else like them, but there are many individuals who try to imitate their celebrity.

Indigo/purple is the spectrum's most complex color and people who prefer it---poets, artists, psychics, mystics and clairvoyants---have one thing in common, they are creative freethinkers and have highly individualistic personalities.

The renowned American psychic Edgar Cayce (1877-1945) comes to mind. People from all walks of life sought him out for readings that revealed dreams and their meaning, soul growth, psychic development, physical healing, prophecy and reincarnation. The readings also described the influence of color. In one of the readings the inquirer asked, "What colors should surround me?" Cayce answered, "Those of gold and blue are healing colors, as is purple, for the body." (Color, Edgar Cayce)

In the painting, "Whirlwind of Lovers" by William Blake (1757-1827) the great English mystic evoked mystical meaning into his oeuvre. His work transcended the ordinary with a spiritually symbolic theme in a painting that appears to send the couple in a whirlwind through a rush of violent color vibrations.

The Indigo ray is symbolically associated in the mind's eye with purple, which is a strong color combining as it does the extremes of the spectrum, warm red and cool blue. Such a dramatic merging of the fiery forces of red and the spiritual aspects of blue are powerful partners in defining personality. Purple may be cast into two distinct types. A substantial purple person is a deep-thinker, artistic and inspired. Someone who is searching for recognition, often the eccentric. Purple people can appear to be aloof and have grandiose ideas about life. Such a person may at times come off as an intellectual snob, but has the education and the talent to achieve a position of authority. Their personality has the ideal temperament well suited for a director of a museum or an art gallery.

When purple is associated with a museum curator it evokes high brow wisdom and the academic knowledge of a definitive period of art or an ancient civilization gleaned by intense research and erudition of the subject.

In contrast the lavender type of person is on a quest to acquire the refined things in life. They are the sensitive types who surround themselves with the social intelligentsia---poets, fashion designers, decorators and patrons of the arts. There is nothing ordinary about their affectation. Choose lavender and you're the type of person who likes to entertain in a grand style with well-orchestrated dinner parties or cocktail soirees.

However, lavender and mauve people often live in a world of fantasy and have a tendency to reinvent themselves above the commonplace of their background. Such is the legend of the designer, Coco Gabriel Chanel who reinvented her heritage with different incarnations from convent waif to world fashion icon. Doesn't matter a bit because lavender people can be counted on to be witty and charming, the perfect host or hostess, or an admired and lovable friend.

Historical Reference

Purple is an ancient dye that has its roots in Egypt, India and Greece. Its name comes from the Latin purpure, the name of a rare shellfish, from which the pigment was originally made. Originally it was hard to produce and only truly wealthy patrons could afford to purchase purple garments. Purple is a flamboyant color that is associated with royalty, pomp and circumstance. It became the royal hue of the Caesars and the nobility ever after wore purple to signify their magnificence and royal status.

"To Wear the Purple" came to mean to be of noble blood; even today the robes of the English royal family are of deep purple velvet. The deep purple amethyst gemstone is often referred to as the "bishop's stone" because this gem is still worn by bishops of the Catholic Church, symbolizing their moral victory over worldly pleasures.

With the invention of aniline dyes in the nineteenth century purple became fashion's first artificial color. Introduced in l856, by the chemist William Henry Perkin (1838-1907) aniline-based dyes made the royal color more widely available, and for a time all ranks of women luxuriated in fashions of dazzling magenta, plum and orchid.

The French claimed it for their own and called it Mauve. It became the rage of the fashion world and Queen Victoria set the trend when she wore a Mauve gown to the International Exhibition in 1862. By the 1890s fashionable women were dedicated to Mauve with a passion.

The Victorians were ideally suited to the mauve-purple craze as it identified with their grand sensibilities and austere code of court etiquette. This filtered down to American standards of Victorianism and the leaders of society, women in New York, Newport, Washington, Lenox and New York were notorious for their penchant for mauve. They were the customers of the French couture and affected the grand style in both their opulent fashions and the home décor in their Gilded Age mansions. Faber Birren explains, "The Mauve Decade tells us of an era when people were neither red nor blue but a combination of both—purple. (Birren, P. 120)

Later these artificial chemical colors fell out of favor and were associated with pretentiousness and vulgarity and for a long time purple was not at all popular. As a matter of fact purplish lips and nails became the vogue along with the (Gothic) Goth look worn by black-clad teenagers and rock musicians. Young women and men, who dyed their hair vibrant purple, had a strong desire to be different and decidedly individualistic. To achieve the full effect, the Goths coordinated their overall appearance for shock value.

One day I asked one of my students, "You are such a pretty young woman, why do you dye your hair and wear all this purple?" She defiantly replied, "I'm making a statement." However, she never could articulate what that statement was all about, but she did accomplish one thing. She stood out in the crowd and looked positively weird, and slightly cadaverous.

Purple can have mysterious and sinister connotations because like black it became synonymous with death and mourning. As such, in individuals who succumb to purple's deep influence, it has the tendency to foster the traits of melancholia and deep depression.

CHAKRA: The Indigo Chakra, (the brow) symbolically relates to the "Spiritual Eye" the center of intuition and clairvoyance through which thoughts and the life force travel. It is at the forehead where the cosmic energy enters the body and sustains all functions of life.

Focusing on the deep blue/purple Indigo Chakra can act as a stimulant as it increases one's ability to become more receptive to messages that may come through meditation. It opens up your ability to visualize and tune up to spirituality, to increase your awareness and ability to tap into new ideas and creativity.

The Indigo vibration can affect thought waves and helps to induce relaxation and decreases anxiety. As such the Indigo Chakra opens the path to realize your spiritual self and connects you to an infinite intelligence.

MEDITATION in a Minute: When life is hectic, spiritual discipline may easily get overlooked or skipped. Time is the problem and most of us question, "How can I be a spiritual seeker and still live in a busy world?"

Edgar Cayce said, "You can make authentic contact with higher consciousness through the third eye, the Indigo Chakra in a single minute." This minute theory should appeal to most of us who declare, "I don't have time." Really? You surely can spare a minute? It's worth a try.

The idea of making spiritual connection in as brief a time as one minute doesn't necessarily imply shortcuts. It requires deep concentration.

First Step: quiet yourself in a private space and start by breathing in and out, very slowly and calmly to center yourself for the one minute meditation.

Step Two: Focus on your breathing, nothing else. As you draw in air your lungs are revitalized. As you exhale the air is cleansed.

Step Three: Then proceed into an actual silent meditation and focus on a personal affirmation, a tool if you will, which could be as brief as a single word (love, health, courage, desire, spiritual fulfillment). Focusing on your affirmation is a method to become more sensitive to what the Edgar Cayce readings call your "individuality" or "higher self."

Step Four: Any meditation should conclude with a period of prayer. Send a positive thought or a blessing directed to people in need and also to yourself. One minute meditation allows us to return to activitity with renewed zest.

Business professionals and any busy hockey mom could achieve powerful results from this brief meditation. You may even want to make a "one minute meditation" part of your daily routine. Caution: Don't expect immediate results you may need to start a routine and patiently practice. Tune into your higher self, be open and receptive. If you get distracted go back to your affirmation and simply wait and be prepared for what comes through the meditation.

MUSIC: Father Castel, Louis-Bertrand Castel, created one of the first actual proposals for a system of color music, in which notes and colors appear simultaneously. A was expressed by the color violet, A sharp, pale violet and B, indigo. French composer Claude Debussy (1862-1918), a radical innovator, dissolved traditional rules into a new language in harmony, rhythm and form, texture, and color. He wrote, "I realize that music is very delicate, and it takes therefore, the soul of its softest fluttering, to catch these violet rays of emotion."

German Composer, Richard Wagner (l813-83) combined poetry, drama, music, song and painting in his music, which critics said, "Raised listeners to states of exalted pleasure."

Audrey Kargere, Ph.D. author "Color and Personality" said, "Only those knowing the spiritual value of music, only those who are able to hear clear-audiently the music of the spheres, are able to comprehend the subtle blends and perfect harmonies of Wagner. Perhaps the spectrum in its entirety seems most appropriate, however, we can assign him a purplish-red."

FASHION: While creative thinkers like artists are drawn to purple for its creative, inspirational qualities, women in general have embraced the purple reign that has filtered down to them through fashion. On the whole fashion has had a love hate relationship with the color.

At one time purple was considered an Old Lady's color. That changed dramatically when Italian designer Emilio Pucci (1914-1992) included purple in his brilliant prints based on medieval Italian banners. The scion of an old aristocratic Tuscan family, Pucci was a born trendsetter and a member of the Italian Olympic ski team. After he wore a classic purple Pucci design with slim black ski pants, the fashion cognoscenti adapted the look worldwide. He established his fashion house in the Palazzo Pucci in Florence, Italy.

To appeal to women's passion for purple, fashion designers made purple their signature color in wearable tints of lilac, amethyst, mauve and lavender. Fashion color consultants have even declared eye-popping 'ultra violet,' the color of the year for 2018, but then on following years, they will select another color to stimulate business. However, while the purple rage is on, indulge! These colors are flattering on most women because they give complexions and eyes a special glow.

RESERVED FOR ROYALTY

Once reserved for royalty, the royal hue also enriches fashion in shades from grape to plum and eggplant. Purple comes full circle and is in favor again for real and would be noble-minded women who dress "on trend."

High-end designers offer new collections that look fabulous in purple. In a full page advertisement, Bloomingdale's called purple, "The New Regal" and featured a lush, double-breasted purple coat with a matching sleeveless turtleneck from Lauren by Ralph Lauren. This rich purple ensemble is radiant and pretty on most any woman, but especially on brunettes and raven-haired beauties.

Career women might opt for a sophisticated statement wearing a darkened violet, an aubergine leather jacket with a black skirt. Black patent accessories complete the professional look. For "on trend" styling carry one of those hugely popular, over-sized, purple leather totes.

Men with noble business aspirations might wear a pale, violet tinted shirt and a purple polka dot tie. It conveys the message that they are smart, approachable and interesting, the kind of man who has a high-minded outlook on life.

By night women can create a highly artistic appearances by wearing three purple colors in three easy pieces. For example, a satin lavender silk blouse under a plum colored velvet jacket with palazzo pants in deep eggplant says you're a fashionista---someone who is ready to party. The look is elegant yet casual and lets you travel on the social circle, from season to season, with cultivated elegance.

On the flirty side of fashion wear a sheer ultra-violet, mini dance frock fashioned in purple chiffon layers and the dress will capture the breeze and attract attention. To be more resplendent in purple choose accessorize such as a fuchsia patent-leather clutch and paint your nails in Chanel's Rodeo Drive "Le Vernis," lavender tint.

Mass fashion producers also go the purple route. Old Navy stores' purple everyday long sleeved, cowl neck T-shirt paired with purple skinny jeans in a deeper tone provides a lot of pizzazz to a casual look for the young-at-heart.

INDIGO: In the corporate world executives with upscale career aspirations need the serious consideration of Indigo to project a professional look. This very dark purplish/navy color is the perfect no nonsense dark shade for business attire to wear by both men and women. With its overtone of heightened intuition imbued in Indigo, it is the way to go, particularly as one climbs the corporate ladder to the board room. Why? Because Indigo will help you to sharpen your mind and make better on-the-spot decisions.

Women may wish to lighten up the Indigo look. For a professional appearance wear a crisp white, tailored cotton blouse with fashionable deep cuffs, which can be turned up on the sleeve of a shapely, Indigo colored blazer.

Men might take a cue from fashion and chose an Indigo cotton sateen shirt with a matching lavender/purple striped tie. I saw this look on a banker recently and it conveyed a very effective impression of "on trend" professionalism.

According to the fashion doyennes, wear indigo and it says you're a deep thinker, an individual who makes snap decisions with proven results. It's the way to go for executives making corporate presentations. It says you are not only a successful presenter but Indigo indicates that you're a creative one as well.

PRODUCTS: Purple has taken a royal spin and not only permeates fashion, but offers consumers new incentives to purchase home furnishings and utility products. No longer are household mops, brooms and dishpans dull, but today they are drenched in color, particularly purple. Watches are also showing off their royal colors. "Mood Indigo wristwatches in deep purple hues make your brown leather band suddenly seem boring," says In Style magazine. "The color makes even the simple watch face into a bolder realm and adds extra panache to of-the-moment cuff design." Fashioned in crocodile, alligator, calfskin and even synthetic fabric, purple watchbands give an artistic twist to keeping time.

The season's prettiest palette comes from soft regal hues in cosmetic product lines. Taking a cue from fashion, makeup is getting the royal treatment with more wearable ultra violet tones. Lavender blush, shimmering lilac eye shadow, electric eggplant eye liner are beauty products that are sophisticated and flattering. "The last time we saw so much purple was in the eighties, the colors were very 'wow'," said a noted makeup artist. She points out that this time around the look is delicate and shimmering. Most women can wear a little lilac or lavender to brighten their complexion.

Just apply it with a light touch and the look is sheer magic, eyes brighten, and inspiration soars. Darken the crease of the eyelet in purple and the look is smoldering chic.

HOME FURNISHINGS: From the lightest lilac to dark plum and electric eggplant, purple the color of royalty, takes interior decorating to a new level of sophistication. A lavender curvilinear leather couch and one fabulous-over-sized, purple wing-back armchair anchors the entrance lobby in a modern. posh apartment building. Take a cue from the decorators and call this décor treatment your own and adapt it in the den or the living room.

In order to appeal to different customer preferences the purple phase has become a good tonic for inspiration and creativity. Just like the interior decorating pros paint the walls of the main room pale aqua and place a plush, purple sofa with matching side chairs on a stylish purple rug, designed by a modern artist, to anchor the space. The ensemble says you're individualist, an inspired decorator, born to the color purple.

To appeal to loft dwellers living in larger spaces the simplicity of white walls may be made more dramatic with oversize furniture. Chose a designer crafted minimalist chair upholstered in a deep purple Kemp fabric. In such a setting, for inspired contemplation, you become the center of attention while guests sit on slick purple Lucite chairs and sip drinks from luminous purple crystal tumblers. Add the exotic touch with a Tibetan rug runner in an ethnic purple floral design.

Kitchen counter color hasn't escaped the purple craze either. Household chefs seeking inspiration might check out the artisan series, which includes a stunning stand mixer in grape with silvery chrome accents. And at the same time you can keep the kids happy with purple swirl lollipops.

EAT YOUR COLORS: You can actually use color to help you to reach a healthy constitution and indigo/purple is high on the list of making healthy choices. Color names often come from fruits and vegetables. Think plums, blackberries and champagne grapes; veggies such as eggplant, purple coleslaw and purple-fringed salad greens.

According to a pharmacy on the Internet, grapes hang in a cluster that has the same shape of the heart. Each grape looks like a blood cell and, it is interesting to note that coincidentally, research shows that dark grapes are also profound heart and blood vitalizing food.

Purple-skinned potatoes are an exceptionally healthy, low-calorie, high-fiber food. According to reliable sources, "Spuds are also a good source of vitamins C and B6, potassium and protein that help to fight heart disease and cancer. "

There's nothing "egg" about eggplant but this purple skinned vegetable is packed with nutrients and a popular ingredient in ratatouille, a French vegetable concoction. It takes inspiration from the spectrum by combining eggplant with zucchini, onions, green peppers, tomatoes and garlic. Served hot it's a stew, served cold it's an appetizer.

Stressed out? Try the purple pick-me-up. It has been proven that just by smelling lavender promotes relaxing brain waves. Put a lavender bouquet in your car and watch stress melt away grid lock confrontation. Family Circle magazine wrote, "Plant an Alzheimer awareness perennial purple garden to help champion Alzheimer research and programs. Such a garden provides a beautiful, fragrant purple display that encourages spiritual renewal."

Plan healthy meals around healthy foods but remember a rainbow combination of colorful veggies is best for a well balanced menu. Example: Toss in a jolt of red tomato to purple fringed salad greens to bring in the life force of the red ray.

Indigo, the ray of spirituality and intuition is the root of color inspiration, and is said to influence the organs of sight, hearing and smelling. Shop wisely and get into an Indigo mood that will open the path to spiritual enlightenment.

TRIVIA: Amethyst is actually a quartz stone that ranges from a very light tint to a deep, deep purple shade. The ancients believed that amethyst had magical powers and dipped in wine it was a love potion. No wonder the amethyst, so utterly romantic, has become the gemstone of choice for modern brides who have made it their own over diamonds.

If you are struggling to make a wise decision, wearing an amethyst sharpens intuition, making it easier for you to make the right choice, especially when it comes to saying "Yes."

Born in February, amethyst is your birthstone. The Greek word means "without drunkenness." The Greeks were aware of the soothing effect of amethyst's rich, purple color for in ancient times it was believed that anyone carrying this stone could not become intoxicated.

Mere mortals have been Born to the Purple. It connotes a royal or exalted birth, someone of imperial, noble, or other high rank. Lady Diana Spencer, the Princess of Wales (1961-1997) was one such creature who brought her fashion celebrity to epic proportions.

Purple Prose is writing that has exaggerated sentiment or pathos especially in an attempt to enlist or manipulate the reader's sympathies. The novel, "The House of Mirth" by famed American author Edith Wharton (1862-1937) comes to mind. She knew how to elicit our sympathies toward the novel's central and fatalistic character Lily Bart. Similarly a Purple Passage in a novel is full of literary devices and effects; marked by excessively ornate rhetoric.

A Purple Patch relates to a brief performance that is unusually stylish and effective. Oscar Wilde (1854-1900) the renowned Irish-born dramatist, poet, humorist and literary wit might personify the kind of personality; he once had what was called, a "Purple Patch" of celebrity. The novels of Romantic fiction writers are full of Purple Passion with its roots in eroticism.

Purple Language is shocking and provocative. In Victorian times the prostitute's wardrobe was synonymous with the dark, sinister aspects of purple and the evils of their dissipated lives were chronicled in literature.

Purple did not always have such a bad name. It represented the height of valor and noble causes. The Order of the Purple Heart (1920-1935) established by the U.S. Armed Forces, was a medal awarded to servicemen wounded in action. During World War II mothers proudly displayed the Purple Heart in their window.

Because of its association with spirituality, it is not surprising that purple is used for ritual, both secular and religious.

Purple seems to imply special refinement, artistic or emotional sensitivity, while mauves and violets are the colors of dreams, visions, of illusions and enchantments, which brings to mind the movie, "The Color Purple," with its nostalgic message and wonderment.

"If you see a tree as blue, then make it

Blue."

-Paul Gauguin

Chapter 3
THE DYNAMICS OF COLOR
Color Psychology

BLUE
Calm and Collected

Steady and Serene
Blue's like a dream

Color of the Sky
Don't question why

It's perfectly clear
If a gray-day's near

Blue is celestial
Timeless 'n Spiritual

It's the Virgin's veil
Uplifting the pale

Calm and collected
Never neglected

Blue waters are calm
Quells tension and alarm

A thirst for knowledge
Blue folks go to college

True blue commands inspection
Loyalty, trust, introspection

Meditate on blue tranquility
Lifting spirit to soliloquy

Mellifluous melodies renew
Count your blessing in Blue

Chapter 3
THE DYNAMICS OF COLOR
Color Psychology

BLUE
Calm and Collected

The sky is blue the sea is too. We see blue in the high plumage of birds and in the extraordinary miracle of the rainbow reflected in the sky as a dawning of hope and prosperity. The constancy of these natural elements makes us feel assured of life's longevity, peace and serenity.

Blue is one of the most popular colors, often associated with wisdom confidence, truth and tranquility. You are drawn to blue because it holds the qualities of gentleness, contentment, patience and composure. Its energy is female. We feel gentled by its soft and soothing, motherly qualities of compassion and caring.

Spirituality has always been associated with the color blue, the symbol of contemplation, prayer and heaven. Ferdinand Hodler, the Swiss artist, who attributed symbolic meaning to color associated Blue with spirituality in his paintings. In religious art we associate blue with the cloak of the Blessed Virgin, symbolic of positive feminine traits.

Mythology also has its female counterparts, such as Minerva, the goddess of wisdom and the arts, who is often portrayed wearing a diaphanous blue gown. Diana, the virgin goddess of the moon and of hunting, and Juno, the ancient Roman Queen of Heaven, the protector of women and marriage, were also clothed in blue.

The ancient alchemists called, Lapis Lazuli (deep blue) the "stone of heaven," as it bestowed upon the wearer an increased sensitivity to higher vibrations. It was sacred to the Egyptians and only the pharaohs and priests were permitted to wear it. As such Egyptian tombs were richly inlaid with Lapis, for it was believed that the stone would protect, guide and cheer the dead as they journeyed to the afterlife.

Blue is a primary color from which other colors may be created and therefore has independent status in the spectrum. According to Edgar Cayce's essay on the meaning of color, blue is the color of the planet Jupiter, which is the ruler of great thoughts and high mindedness.

On the wavelength of blue your creativity soars and the ability to communicate flows in peaceful conversations that exchange ideas with sensible solutions. Trusting and an excellent team player, blue personalities command respect and are usually persons in authoritative positions like managers, teachers and homemakers who initiate new ideas, but give credit where credit is due.

Blue personalities are admired for their peaceful negotiations and fair play tactics, and that is why people are attracted to them.

BLUE HISTORY: True blue was unknown until the Middle Ages when it was reserved for royalty and works of art. Blue dye was rare and only available from Lapis Lazuli minerals and the woad plant, and was a valued commodity. Later the stronger indigo dye came from Europe and during the Rococo period, both vivid and light blues turn up in paintings and textiles alike.

Then in the nineteenth century along came denim, made from indigo-dyed cotton and fashion has made this fabric its number one choice in casual clothing . Blue even segued over to home furnishings.

AMERICA'S FAVORITE COLOR: Alas the world would be a very sad place without the blue of the sea and sky, the streams and lakes. Restful and cool, blue the second primary pigment, has made its way into mainstream America as its favorite color. Perhaps that's because the average brain secretes tranquilizing hormones when blue is present in the environment. Research shows that looking at blue actually lowers the physiological signs of stress. In general most everyone likes some tint or shade of blue in their clothing or home environment.

Color names conjure up familiar images. Think chalk blue, powder blue, ice blue, sky blue, baby blue, blue jay, China blue, Delft blue, bluebell or cornflower blue. Darker blues like navy, cobalt, royal blue, marine blue and middy blue connote authority and command respect.

Blue represents new things, new relationships and invigorating ideas coming to the fore. It fosters a thirst for knowledge and self-expression and links the higher mind to intuitive understanding, and symbolizes peace, tranquility and relaxation. Sensitive and self-controlled a true blue personality is affectionate, faithful, sensitive and loves to draw new people into the framework of their social life. Pick blue and it will make everyone feel at ease in your presence.

With its non-threatening attitude, navy blue is considered the color of loyalty and dependability. It is no wonder, therefore, that police officers' and airline pilots' uniforms, and bankers' suits subscribe to wearing this color as a badge of integrity and reliability.

However, blue like all the other colors, has both positive and negative associations. Troubled or restless people should bring blue into their environment to absorb its calming qualities and to restore composure and patience. Next time you're having trouble sleeping focus on Wedgwood blue. This soothing, calm-induced color can bring you down from a high wired stress level and help to induce sleep, so you slumber like a babe. Children also sleep better in a Wedgwood blue room ,which can calm their restlessness.

The tonalities of blue from light to dark can have different positive or negative meaning. Falling into a deep blue funk, for example, can signal a state of melancholia.

A penchant for too much blue could possibly mean that you are using blue as a scapegoat, to release you from the realities of life's trials and tribulations. To compose with satiny verse poets also describe blue. The romantic English poet, John Keats (1795-1821) wrote about the color BLUE in this sonnet:

Blue! Gentle cousin of the forest-green Married to green in all the sweetest flowers. Forget-me-Not,--the blue bell,--and, that Queen of secrecy, the violet.

FASHION: Blue comes in a multi-faceted range of pale tints as well as bright and deep, dark shades. It is considered the most flattering color for most people to wear. Everyone likes some sort of blue, especially blue denim jeans and jackets. Perhaps that explains the popularity of blue as America's favorite color.

The dynamics of blue varies dramatically with each tint or shade. Wear a powder blue outfit and it says you're a dreamer, someone who is delicate and innocent. It is usually the choice of a creative thinker or an artist. In wardrobe planning Blue offers ever-changing opportunities to express your mood each day.

The many tints and shades of blue have become a basic wardrobe choice. If you coordinate a Powder Blue wool jacket with a chocolate brown turtle neck sweater and matching skirt it says you're a creative fashion forward thinker.

However, when you wear forest green pants with the same powder blue jacket, it says that you are an 'on trend' individual who is adventurous and high minded.

Choose Electric Blue, and like the blue of an electric spark, it lets everyone know that you have an electrifying personality. People are drawn to you because you are a thoughtful, loyal and a responsive friend. You're a good communicator and individuals eagerly listen to your every word.

BUSINESS ATTIRE: A dark navy blue suit or pantsuit has become a basic for on-the-job attire. It is a good interview choice, too, because it tells the employer that you are the type of employee who can be relied upon to efficiently pull the task through to its successful completion.

Women can lighten up the professional navy look with a strawberry pink silk blouse that says you are warm-hearted and rather approachable. Similarly, men may choose a cobalt blue shirt with a yellow and cobalt blue white striped necktie to bring a touch of originality to their outfit. It conveys the message that while such a person is reliable and trustworthy, they are also friendly and converse on a social level.

Pin stripes, checks, herringbone and glen plaid fabrics, borrowed from men's wear, give women a tailored status and the tenacity to escalate up the corporate ladder.

Natty Nautical Blue takes its cue from the yachting set and women have claimed it for their own in classic blazers, tailored suits and trench coats with brass button accents.

Noted color authority Carlton Wagner, founder and director of the Wagner Institute of Color Research knew about the power of blue. He said, "A lawyer or substitute teacher should wear navy to command respect. " Wagner also stated that "If you have to pick the wardrobe for your defense lawyer heading into court, and choose anything but blue, you deserve to lose the case."

In fashion they say that dark blue is the new black. To add unforgettable drama to evening wear, choose a dark blue satin cocktail suit with a matching star studded sequined bustier. Such a sensuous look solicits compliments for your innovative and creative coordination.

An electric blue strapless taffeta evening gown with a matching lace bolero complements your inner blue confidence and puts you in the special occasion limelight.

HOME FURNISHINGS: Blue in the home environment creates a very soothing ambiance and relieves the tension brought on by computer driven home offices. It is one of the coolest colors in the spectrum and, as such, can make you feel calm, cool and connected.

Walls painted light blue bring in the sky and light up the interior with harmonious peace and calming vibrations. High wired individuals release tension and seemingly lessen their anxieties in such a room. Why? Because blue is on the cool side of the color palette and, as such, it gentles one's nerves and settles emotions.

A formal room painted pale blue has livable charm and when you combine blue with yellow, which is at the opposite side of the color wheel, the comfort factor is enhanced. Indulge your senses and chose a soft yellow couch and a pair of matching side chairs upholstered in a blue Toile de Jouy pictorial print to anchor the room's tranquility. Then add accessories on a coffee table, such as yellow tulips in a Delft blue vase. Yellow candles in blue glass candlesticks add drama as well. Then, too, add Blue Toile de Jouy pillows to enhance the cheerful ambiance.

People sleep peacefully in a Wedgwood blue bedroom. Go easy, however, because the intensity of a completely blue bedroom can make us so comfortable we may tend to oversleep. To counteract this tendency, add the jolt of another color, like tangy tangerine bed linens and decorative toss pillows.

Research has acknowledged that babies cry less in a blue room. Then, too, science has proven that premature babies' survival rate is higher in a blue infused light.

Blue is an expansive color and when you want to make a small room seem larger a blue décor seemingly creates a larger venue . Instead of coming into a white room, dark blue painted walls can make a dining room more inviting. For instance, a white dinner table and matching chairs sets the stage for a Royal Blue area rug underneath, while adding sheer pale blue chiffon window curtains will create an airy ambiance. To enhance a "little bit of blue heaven" to the decorative scheme, and just to add a jolt of serenity, paint one of the walls a lighter blue, the perfect background for hanging impressionistic blue artwork.

Blue is a natural agent that creates a spa-like feeling for adults with aquatic serenity. Even the most energetic child or antsy student will calm down in a blue room, and mothers do too. For a nautical ambiance, opt for a shipshape room with trompe l'oeil portholes on blue walls. To enhance the seaworthy theme throughout a child's room, choose pale blue, cool-looking nautical bed linens. Nautical motif tabletop accessories and toss pillows complete the natty look.

According to noted color authority Carlton Wagner when schoolroom walls were changed from orange-and-white to blue, students' blood pressure dropped, their behavior improved and learning comprehension soared

Blue with its connection to spirituality is used in rooms where people meditate and peaceful contemplation is desired.

Dieters need only to choose blue for their kitchen to see pounds shed like magic. Why? Studies have shown that blue curbs hunger and makes it easier for you to stick to a healthy diet plan.

Enamel cooking pots, other kitchen counter appliances and utensils are another blue way to become less and less food conscious. What's more, people tend to curb their intake of food when they dine in a blue kitchen.

PRODUCTS: Color identification is a clear key to a product's success. No wonder laundry detergents come in a variety blue, blue and white, and blue and orange packages that consumers perceive as trustworthy and powerful cleaning products.

Images of exotic resort scenes on health and cosmetic packaging lure us to purchase spa products that promise to soothe, easy and eliminate tension. Then too, blue-tinted health drinks promise to deliver energy in a bottle, while acai berries suggest the slimming benefits of blue that curbs appetites. Best diet advice; chose blue dinner plates to cool down interest in food and discourage overeating.

Blue Dog Nutrition packages its natural ingredient dog food products in blue packaging, and the "Blue" logo says "Be True, Feed Blue." Perhaps they are alluding to "True Blue" a phrase that represents a person, and in this case a product of true blue quality and loyalty.

INSPIRATION: "It is the Heavens, the sky that gives us inspiration. It tells us that we can be more than what we have ever thought to be," says a Native American healer. She writes and interprets Native American culture through the natural elements: Water, Earth, Fire and Sky.

For example, Look at the night sky, it gives us hope, the drive to continue steadfast on life's plane and it enables us to enter into the darkness of ourselves and to see who we really are. By gazing above you can enter into the sky's darkness, and discover who you are, and what you can become and all the endless potential that exists.

The Universe is a wonderful ally, bringing us wisdom empowerment and gifts. Just gaze at the night sky's brilliance and ask for the fulfillment of your heart's desire. The sky is freedom. It allows us to be still and connect to the Universe where we can be enlightened, empowered and inspired to think outside the box, not allowing anything or anyone to restrict who we are and who we can become."

The velvety black sky portends a powerful message that empowers the believer. Why not try it, next time on a dark, star studded night look to the sky for inspiration. On a lighter note, you can also get a free energy booster by looking at the sun right outside your window, because it shines blue light which empowers us with energy and alertness.

CHAKRA: The Blue Chakra (the throat, nose, ears and mouth) is beneficial for all throat and speech problems. When Susan 28, suffered from a scratchy throat she gently wrapped a blue scarf around her neck for relief. The voice, the center of self-expression, is linked to the Blue Chakra. (Guerin, Healing Color)

Therefore, if you are having a problem getting your point across, blue is the perfect meditation color of choice for overcoming all sorts of communication quandaries. Blue is a relaxant and is excellent choice when you are overly excited or have bouts of anxiety. For that reason professional lecturers often focus on blue to settle their platform jitters.

Blue is also the vibration of truth and when you meditate on the throat chakra it will aid in developing this quality. The Blue Chakra is composed of intellect and also links the higher mind to intuitive understanding. It fosters a great desire for knowledge and self-expression with the constancy of loyalty and trust.

MUSIC: Blue is represented by "G" note on the C musical scale and the vocal sound Ee. In their book, the *Color Compendium* authors Hope and Walsh state that Wassily Kandinsky insisted that color influences the soul, "Color is the keyboard, the eyes are the hammer, the soul is the piano of many strings."

Audrey Kargere in *Color and Personality* said, "Chopin became known as the mirror of aspirations, thwarted desires and ambitions of the intelligentsia of his day. On the whole Chopin advocated the transmuting of baser elements and emotions to a higher level of consciousness---to service. This high spirituality indicates the color blue."

Russian composer, Alexander Scriabin (1872-1915) was the first composer to combine metaphysics with symphonic music. Writing in *Classical Music*, general editor John Burrows OBE, alludes to the composer's interest in mystical philosophy as follows: "Scriabin wrote a complete part for "Tastiera per Luce," "("keyboard of lights"), which would then flood the performance space with different colored lights according to which combination of keys was pressed. The work was intended to be an early--perhaps first--example of a multimedia performance. Prometheus, the Poems of Fire was the last of Scriabin's five symphonies. It is a striking work, and contains many moments of sensuous orchestration with bold and other-worldly harmony." It is said that the unusual quality of the unearthly music reaches the souls who listen. Scriabin's color was deep blue.

To each listener the energy of Blue in music provides different personal experiences. Its wavelength of spiritual renewal in liturgical works transcends the ordinary and transports us to higher realms of contemplation. Then, too, contemporary and modern pieces heighten our awareness of what is new, fashionable or risqué. The next time you listen to music take time to note how the melody lifts your enjoyment beyond the cares and frustrations of daily experiences.

It is interesting to note that while blue can be lofty and inspiring the color is also associated with a deep, dark rhythm called, "The Blues," which is a common description for Jazz-age music.

The book, Classical Music tells us, "The premiere of "Rhapsody in Blue" in 1924 propelled American composer, George Gershwin (1898-1937) into the history books as the man who first brought jazz into the concert hall. The obvious jazzy elements in the score have obscured the distinctly, Jewish tinge in the melodies, some of which recall synagogue chants."

EAT YOUR COLOR: There's a lot to be said about eating your blue fruits and veggies. Blueberries for one are packed with benefits such as antioxidants that reduce fat in your arteries. A born fighter against bad cholesterol it's wise to get your daily helping of blueberries on cereal or scoop those berries into low fat yogurt in the blender for a frothy, delicious drink.

Getting forgetful? Researches found that by eating a cup of blueberries a day improved people's recall. Why? Credit goes to berry pigments that activate the area of the brain that controls memory. You can also drink blueberry juice for the same reason. Blueberries are also an essential nutrient for good eyesight.

The Acai fruit has been revered by South American Indians for its legendary energizing health benefits. Acai has come mainstream as another choice by health-conscious Americans as a refreshing beverage or to mix it with bananas as a nutritious meal.

When shopping consider adding to your basket blue tinged potatoes, blue fringed salad greens, bluish plums and bilberries. Advice from the experts: Don't discard the skin of vegetables; you might be throwing away valuable nutrients. Just buy a veggie brush and clean the outer surface. Potassium, for example, a mineral that promotes regular heartbeats and muscle contractions can be found in the skin of potatoes.

TRIVIA: Blue has had a long history associated with Jazz. We hear of the Blue Note and the Blues, a characteristic feature in music marked by the frequent occurrence of blue notes. On rainy days when a certain melancholy overtakes us, we have "The Blues."

We give titles to nobility and call them Blue Bloods. They invest in low risk, Blue Chip stocks and get their names listed in the social registry, The Blue Book. Let's not forget the famed Tiffany blue box, which incidentally is more aqua than blue, but people seem to call it Tiffany Blue. Then there's the Blue State, which identifies with either democratic or republican preferences.

Blue Collar workers identify with their trade as longshoremen, mechanics or miners and they don't look forward to Blue Monday when they have to return to work. We hope instead for something Out of the Blue, like an inheritance or a lottery winning. When someone disappears we say they've gone somewhere, Into the Blue, vanished beyond the Blue Horizon.

Blue is an ambivalent color. Its meaning depends on the word association. It can be somewhat obscene or indecent like a Blue Joke or Blue Film. And we don't want to meet the fairy tale character, Bluebeard under any blue circumstances.

We try to discipline our children until we are Blue in the Face and squeeze into our Blue Jeans to look fashionable. The Blue Plate Special, a modest meat and vegetable meal, emerged during the Great Depression (1930s) in inexpensive restaurants. I wonder if in today's economic conditions the Blue Plate might reappear on the menu. The Antiques Road Show experts will probably tell you that Delftware, the white earthenware with blue over-glaze decoration is highly collectible.

Blue themes have proliferated in poetry and prose. John Keats' sonnet BLUE , mentioned earlier, reminds us of blue in nature, "Blue! gentle cousin of the forest-green, married to green in all the sweetest flowers,--Forget-me-not,--the blue bell."

Different cultures also look to nature for color names. In travel we visit the Blue Grass region in central Kentucky known for its fields of seemingly blue grass. And we'll hop an Acela train that take us to our destination like a Blue Streak. Blue laws that still exist in some states forbid drinking, working or dancing on Sunday. For the highest honor there is the Blue Ribbon, the first prize awarded in a contest.

Spanish artist, Pablo Picasso (1881-1973) was the dominant figure of the 20th-century art world. In 1904 he settled in Paris, which was the inspiration for his most prolific and acclaimed,"Blue Period," during which he painted--with blue predominant--the city's prostitutes and destitutes.

To show your true love give your lady or favorite beau a blue sapphire. It says what's honestly in your heart because the sapphire represents sincerity. If you are an Amish lass, paint your gate blue, it'll let everyone know you are available.

Then "if music be the food of love" (Twelfth-Night by William Shakespeare) let's not forget American composer Samuel Barber (1910-81) whose lyrical romantic works recall his gift for flowing, memorable melody lines. Like the poetic lament, "Tell me oh blue, blue sky, why did we part?," which reaches to the sky for answers. It is said that he composed the song after a friend's suicide.

To bring awareness of diabetes, November 14th is World Diabetes Day and Blue Lights will shine on iconic monuments all over the world, including the Australia's Sydney Opera House, Rio de Janeiro's Christ the Redeemer statue, and at the top of the Empire State Building in New York City. Turning on Blue Light awareness supports the 246 million people world-wide living with it.

Born in September, you can claim Sapphire as your birth stone, which represents sincerity and looks stunning with a summer tan. If all else fails to give you a better outlook on life, put on blue-tinted glasses and see the world in peace and harmony.

"The chief function of color should be to serve expression."

-Henri Matisse

THE DYNAMICS OF COLOR
Color Psychology

AQUAMARINE
Aquatic Visions

Aqua's lively and serene
Part water and blue marine

Conjure up languid days
Spa visits 'n healthy stays

Restful and rejuvenating
Aqua ray's invigorating

Take the plunge, Immerse
In dazzling pools disperse

Reduce tension, slimming
Visualize aqua swimming

In pools of Mediterranean
View the lush terrarium

Transparency in blue/green
Aqua crowns Neptune's queen

A gift of the sea's selection
Sailors pride its protection

Add spaciousness to living
Cool Aqua is so forgiving

Makes life a softer hue
Aqua dreams heal and renew.

Chapter 4
THE DYNAMICS OF COLOR
Color Psychology

AQUAMARINE
Aquatic Visions

Imagine what happens when we go to the beach and plunge into the sea. Our senses come in tune with the 'aqua' (water) and 'mare' (the sea), after which Aquamarine is named. The beauty of the sky and its reflection on sunlit waters reminds us of the Mediterranean and Caribbean underwater blues. From aqua (water) emerges the beauty of the aquamarine stone in a beautiful range of light blue colors. It's appeal spans age categories and is an equally attractive and youthful color for both men and women.

Men however, might take a cue from nautical folklore. Like a gift from the sea, aquamarines were the gemstone of choice given by Neptune to his mermaids. It is interesting to note that aquamarine has become popular as an engagement ring, because according to old tradition, it promises a happy marriage. Then, too, women who wear aquamarine are said to garner joy and wealth in the bargain.

Aquamarine is a color that requires nurturing as it has a chameleon personality that changes from blue to a transparent bluish-green. Its duplicity has positive virtue because aquamarine gives us the dual benefits of blue that inspires honesty and loyalty with green for balance and harmony. The light blue gemstone arouses feelings of sympathy, trust, harmony and friendship. What's more, it complements almost any skin type and makes eyes sparkle.

HISTORY: The ancients revered gemstones for their color and used them as healing amulets, that were either ground to a fine pulp or dipped in water as remedies for a variety of ailments. Ancient people put great faith in the healing benefit of the aquamarine's power to heal. Modern day practitioners, who specialize in gemstone therapy, similarly suggest that client's wear aquamarine amulets to ward off certain ailments or mental stress. Interesting to note that men, the titans of finance and high tech, seeking a deeper purpose in their life, are now spending thousands on crystals and gem therapy.

Clients are also advised to carry the gemstone with them at all times to continue the healing process and to maintain its benefits. Women are particularly attracted and susceptible to gemstone therapy. It is appealing to most married women because it is believed that the gemstone, aquamarine, helps strengthen ties with everyone, particularly their husband. As for a lagging romance, aquamarine is believed to rekindle romance in long married couples. As for singles, this gemstone will help to keep romance aglow.

Career women who want to become a better team player may favor aquamarine for the same strengthening reason. Wearing it will improve relationships with co-workers.

FASHION: Aquamarine is a delicate color and as such it can create a sweet and youthful appearance. A bolder concept is the quintessential Art Deco color formula, aquamarine and black, which was popular in enameled jewelry, geometric textile prints and fashions of the 1920's and 1930's.

The term 'Art Deco' emanated from the Paris Exposition Internationale des Arts Decoratifs et Industriels Modernes, which was held in Paris, France in 1925, and the influence of modernism quickly spread throughout the world. The eclectic style conveys the innovative spirit of the interwar years, the period between World War I and World War II, when Paris was the quintessential center of the fashion world.

A luminary such as Gabrielle "Coco" Chanel was an influential designer of the Art Deco period. She was the first Haute Couture couturier to introduce costume jewelry, which imitated genuine gems. Such innovation became the rage when she showcased her stunning, enameled, aquamarine, wide cuff bracelets embellished with a Maltese cross to complement her fashion collections.

Most everyone can wear a classic aquamarine outfit because it has a split personality. Blondes with a great tan would look aquatic and gorgeous. Brunettes look more dramatic as if they were born on a tropical island.

Wear an aquamarine silk swing jacket with white silk shantung cigarette-tight stretch pants, and it says you're an adventurous clam digger looking for a mate. A lightweight aquamarine wool twin-sweater-set worn with matching floral printed shorts has island-hopping flair. In such an outfit you will look approachable and garner admiring glances.

The mother of the bride can show off her stunning silver hair and creamy complexion wearing an elegant aquamarine silk gown drizzled with opalescent crystals, illuminating her path, just like a modern mermaid.

HOME FURNISHINGS: You may not own a beach house but aquamarine can create an ambiance that will allow you to escape into your own dream vacation. Rooms painted in aquamarine are always cool, calm and refreshing and make any space look seemingly larger. Such an environment is dreamy and reminds us of vacation vistas lounging on the French Riviera with the aqua blue ocean in the horizon.

Invite guests to sit on a sofa slip-covered in aquamarine and add crisp white accent pillows fringed with opalescent crystal beads and the feeling is like living on a tropical island--- cool, breezy, fresh and inviting. Add two large side chairs in an aquamarine and white, bold check print with just a dash of red, and the room vicariously becomes an instant vacation simulator. To further the theme select white framed artwork with sail boat scenes, picturesque seascapes or underwater subjects and the décor conjures up serene comfort in a cool oasis of aquamarine contentment.

In a dining room the highly changeable, blue-green character of aquamarine finds its most interesting expression woven in silk shantung for seat covers, table runners and napkins. Depending upon the lighting system, the fabric reflects either blue or green overtones in a very restful and inviting setting.

Taking color cue from the ocean you can feel island happy right at home. For instance, aquamarine painted walls can transform the bathroom into a spa like oasis of rest and rejuvenation. Add translucent aquamarine candles and indulge your senses with an aquatic fragrance that reminds you of a stroll on a windswept beach.

PRODUCT: Spa products come to mind when I think of aquamarine. It is the most natural association linking water and marine to products that portend to soothe, heal and rejuvenate. An aquamarine-infused muscle soak, for example, is considered a therapeutic spa powder that releases tension due to stress or overexertion. It leaves us feeling calm, tranquilized and renewed.

Then, too, when tiny aquamarine beads are dissolved in bath water, it refreshes and revitalizes with sea breeze aroma. On another note, aquamarine-infused drinks are promoted as the elixir of power to re-energize and keep us moving forward to compete in the race, or better yet, to see a project through with successful results.

We are so fascinated aquamarine that we put a large sea shell to our ear to hear the symphony of the sea or light sea shell shaped candles to illuminate the way to an imagined resort island.

DRINK AQUA: Water 'Aqua ' is the source of a healthy, vibrant life. My Caycean chiropractor, Dr. Scott Keller reminds me every time I visit him, "Ms Guerin have you been drinking 8 glasses of water a day? I can tell today that by the condition of your body that, "You are not drinking enough water."

According to Edgar Cayce's recipe for a health, it is important to remember to drink enough water daily to keep your system hydrated and cleansed.

Like many other people I also find it difficult to drink those eight glasses of water, but I've improved my intake and feeling ever so much better. Why? Because water detoxifies our body, it flushes out impurities, and in this inexpensive way, it has the added benefit of helping us to shed pounds and lose weight. So drink up, be healthy, it's your life. Make it an aquatic one. By the way, showers are another therapeutic use of water. While hot water is relaxing it should be followed by short cold shower to stimulate and energize your body.

The sound of water trickling and bubbling in an indoor fountain is not only soothing and relaxing, but the water releases negative ions that wash away airborne germs.

TRIVIA: Since ancient Greek times sailors knew the power of the aquamarine stone and carried it on their sea voyages as a charm for protection and courage. In this computer driven society gemstone practitioners similarly recommend aquamarine to their clients to help them to feel safe, protected and open-hearted.

Born in March you can claim aquamarine as your own and make the most of this heavenly gemstone's duplicity. It reflects the purity of wisdom with the aqua vibes of peaceful contemplation.

According to Faber Birren, "If your color is blue-green like aquamarine, you have a sensitive nature, and probably come from refined and intellectual parents, had a well-tutored childhood or achieved refinement entirely on your own." Well, that statement is particularly interesting, because it says that you are capable of managing your own affairs and that bodes well for women moving in a career path that demands quick and precise decisions. Then, too, you take admiration for granted. Such is the privilege of the aquamarine personality. Lucky You!!!

"A turquoise given by a loving hand carries with it happiness and good fortune."

-Arabic Proverb

Chapter 5
THE DYNAMICS OF COLOR
Color Psychology

TURQUOISE
Healing Powers

Gems create Earth's pleasures
Gives us Turquoise treasures

Ancient cultures knew its worth
Taking Turquoise from the earth

Turquoise with veins of brown
Worn by a princess as a crown

Wrought in awesome jewelry
Silver streaks light the way

Talisman of Indian nations
Tweaks brilliant imagination

Youthful and forgiving
Turquoise improves living

Energizes romantic notions
Even with out potions

A gemstone of healing power
Dispels a springtime shower

Turquoise by any other name
Is not genuine, not the same

Intrinsic value is in the stone
Created by earth for you alone.

Chapter 5
THE DYNAMICS OF COLOR
Color Psychology

TURQUOISE
Healing Powers

Turquoise is unmistakably one of the most beautiful, natural stones, and by association with the Southwest, where it is mined, it has become a highly appreciated stone for its legendary qualities.

When we think of the Southwest we are often reminded of the paintings of the American artist, Georgia O'Keeffe (1887-1986), known for her semi abstract paintings of larger-then-life flowers and desert landscapes that evoke the bleak territory.

Once you have seen a desert sunset it is forever etched into memory as an unforgettable experience of blazing reds, orange and golden sun woven into a turquoise rainbow, just like the blankets created by native craftsmen.

American Indians revered the natural wonders of sky, water and earth in mystical native designs that decorated clothing, art work, bold blanket patterns and earthen clay pots, which are highly coveted collectibles today.

The Pueblo, Navajo and Apache tribes cherished turquoise for its amuletic use and the Apache believed the stone could afford the archer dead aim. All the Pueblo groups, which include Zuni, Hopi, and Rio Grande people, have used turquoise for ornamentation. With the increased availability of smaller stones and improved lapidary tools, the Zuni jewelry was oriented towards turquoise with silver.

Since ancient times Turquoise was a highly treasured stone for it symbolized the azure of the sky captured in a bluish-green stone. It was believed to have powerful healing qualities to prevent or cure a variety of illness or ailments with earthbound wellness. Since turquoise combines both blue and green it has the calming benefit of blue with the healthful balance of green. Therefore it is considered both cool and relaxing. Wear it often, as it claims to calm headaches.

Exotic and mystical turquoise, sometimes with thin reddish veins or flecks running through the stone, was thought by ancient people to have traces of the blood of Mother Earth and therefore was highly respected for its folkloric symbolism.

HISTORY: Turquoise was first found in Turkestan, also known as Turkestan or Kazakhstan, located in a vast region in West and central Asia and was known as "Turkish stone." The name turquoise derives from the equivalent combining of Turk + oise, which is the feminine form of ois.

In many great cultures of antiquity, turquoise jewels have adorned the rulers of ancient Egypt, the Aztecs, Persia, Mesopotamia and China. It is considered to be one of the oldest gems and was first introduced to Europe through Turkey.

Egyptian royalty wore many layered rows of turquoise and earthen red beads in wide gold collars that adorned their bronzed body. The gold death masks of the Pharaohs, like Tutankhamen, were inlaid with turquoise stones and they were buried wearing turquoise jewelry to enrich their afterlife.

PERSONALITY: "Narcissism and self-love are deep rooted in blue-green," wrote Faber Birren. He explains, "This is by no means a fault, because Freud regarded narcissism as 'the purest and truest feminine type. Can you identify such a woman? She is the the kind of person who seldom gives much love; instead, her need is to be loved."

A man who favors blue-green may also find himself unable to maintain a relationship and truly love anyone else but himself. You might want to avoid this kind of individual, and perhaps reconsider getting involved at all. When it comes to love, such a man usually keeps a strong control on his emotions. Need I say more?

However, on the plus side, and much to their favor, men who favor turquoise are neat, well-groomed, sharp-witted and successful in business. This kind of person is likely to inspire envy and annoyance because of his apparent conceit. In the business sector, however, his name is usually on the last rung of the popularity pole.

Betty Wood in the book, *The Healing Power of Color* wrote, "Those choosing turquoise often drive themselves hard and there is occasionally quite a state of turmoil under that outwardly cool exterior."

FASHION: When it comes to the Southwest and gemstone Turquoise, I call to mind a very special woman, an advocate for American Indian culture, the socialite, Mary Millicent Rogers (1902-1953). She adapted American Indian fashions and stylized them as her own individualistic creations, which she wore with dramatic turquoise silver jewelry. A passion for life's aesthetic pleasures inspired a journey that led her to the beautiful and historic land of Taos, New Mexico, where its scenic beauty, tranquility, ideal climate and Native American culture, sparked the genius in her creativity.

Rogers was known to the world as an American beauty and fashion icon. Her originality was legendary and her style influence reached far and wide into women's wardrobes. She believed the Southwestern Indian culture was a precious part of America's heritage that had to be recognized and preserved.

Millicent was instrumental in popularizing this rich culture, not only through her own jewelry and fashion creations, but through her lifetime collections of indigenous art. Paying tribute to Native American artifacts, turquoise and silver jewelry, nearly 1,000 rare pieces, largely collected by Rogers herself, are exhibited in the Millicent Rogers Museum in Taos, New Mexico. Now, more than ever, it is easy to recognize how instrumental she was in popularizing this rich culture.

The serious career woman may not be able to fully embrace Southwestern style for daytime or business attire. However, a turquoise silk blouse with a dark navy or black suit lights up your face and says you have poise and convey at the same time a professional appearance.

Turquoise evening wear evokes entrance-making drama. A strapless silk shantung party dress in deep turquoise, for example, will look elegant and stunning and is especially attractive when worn with traditional silver and turquoise jewelry.

Women who dare to show off their curves might wear a strapless, form-fitting bustier in shiny turquoise satin with a black velvet fishtail evening skirt. It reflects a movie star image and the height of sophistication. Wear a turquoise gemstone dog collar and you are what the French call, "Tres Chic."

Business Attire: A deep blue-green shade, fashionably called 'teal,' is a flattering color for most complexions and conveys lively sophistication. When a silk turquoise blouse, underneath a teal wool blazer, is paired with a black skirt it is appropriate for office attire and gives the impression that you are confident and an efficient executive. Add turquoise/silver jewelry and it will brighten your career apparel.

On a crisp autumn day, toss a terracotta and turquoise paisley shawl over your shoulder and the contrast will give a soft, feminine flair to the ensemble.

Take inspiration from the fine jewelers and shop for vintage jewelry collectibles like a diamond-like rhinestone and turquoise necklace to give your wardrobe special panache. Brooches, leaf earrings and Victorian pieces may also be found in thrift shops or offered for sale on Ebay.

FURNISHINGS: If you're the type of person who likes to identify a room with a particular culture then Southwestern is a practical choice. It is particularly adaptable for a bedroom or family room in a resort cabin or beach house.

In the city, looking at a painting of turquoise sunset helps to recharge one's sensitivities to the health restoring benefits of the spectrum colors. Such a painting also provides eye relief from working on the computer screen. Then, too, getting up from the computer or TV and doing nothing for at least ten minutes will re-invest energy into your body.

To create a Southwestern room ambiance contrast a light color against a dark color by painting window frames and architectural trims in a terracotta tint and walls in a deeper, warm terracotta shade. This inviting contrast is the perfect background to offset the room with a rich turquoise, faux-teal-leather sofa and matching side chairs. Accent accessories might include Pueblo blankets or toss pillows in turquoise imprinted with Navaho motifs. Wood cabinet furniture will add a cozy southwestern feel to the room.

Then too, accessories usually add interest to the room, like a matching set of turquoise glass vases in different sizes and heights. Arrange them together by a window for a dramatic light-catching arrangement that sends beams of turquoise throughout the room. For a truly artistic approach, choose a glass sculpture centerpiece, inspired by the famed sculptures by artist Dale Chihuly, founder of the Pilchuck Glass School in Seattle, WA.

When you place such a centerpiece on the coffee table it garners compliments. Granted you may not afford an original Chihuly, nor can I, but affordable artistic glass sculptures are available in the table top or decorative arts section of major department and specialty stores to meet most budgets.

Mission style wood framed furniture has that one-of-a-kind craftsmanship look and when it is upholstered in Navajo turquoise blanket patterns it conveys casual country cabin style. Such a decorating scheme promotes balance and harmony and reinforces a cozy environment.

PRODUCTS: Color associated with a calming ambiance are especially important in maintaining customer loyalty. Turquoise is a good color for beauty parlors as it creates an attractive and relaxing setting where women tend to linger longer to enjoy the respite from their daily life.

Turquoise is also a good color for a Spa as it conjures up the impression of calm comfort in a meditative setting.

It is interesting to note that the negative effect resulted when a successful spa in Switzerland switched from traditional turquoise and white to maroon and gray. Customer attendance declined and the spa lost its popularity. So the message is loud and clear. If you have a perfectly consumer recognized turquoise and white formula why change it?

TURQUOISE in the Market: Did you ever wonder why some food stands out more attractively when they are displayed against a turquoise background? Well the supermarkets know a think or two about presentation, because meat looks redder, more fresh and appetizing.

HEALTH: The calming quality of a blue-green turquoise stone is often used in holistic medicine to treat patients who suffer from panic attacks. Walls painted light turquoise, for example, have a soft feminine feel while deeper shades of turquoise are effective in cooling down disruptive personalities.

In hospitals turquoise or blue-green is often the preferred color in the operating theater and is the color of choice for garments. The blue of spirituality links with the healing powers of green and counteracts the glare of high intensity lights in the operating room. Hospital administrators would do well to study the healing properties of color, which could help to promote the healing process. When patients look up at the ceiling in their recovery room, if it was painted a light turquoise, it may psychologically suggest blissful recovery.

TRIVIA: Ladies be aware. The color of the turquoise stone deteriorates if it absorbs hairspray or cosmetics. To protect this semi-precious stone, for years to come, it is advisable to put on your turquoise jewelry after your beauty routine.

Born in December your birthstone is turquoise. According to soothsayers you can get ahead in any situation by wearing turquoise. It is revered as a stone that banishes negativity and opens the path to successful encounters and the fulfillment of aspirations. No wonder turquoise and silver jewelry is so popular worn by both men and women.

The ancients thought that the turquoise stone could cure illness and recommended that amulets be worn or carried in a pocket. Not feeling quite yourself? Turquoise calms the mind and is cooling to the nervous system. It allows you to take command of any situation with confidence and clarity.

Turquoise links up to the mind and wearing this gemstone is said inspire new ideas and creativity. The two colors of blue and green that make up this color are beneficial to us all; peace, harmony and balance.

Then there is the Turquoise Coast in Turkey where the blue-green waters run deep in the clear depths of the Mediterranean. Modern adventurers take the "Blue Voyage" cruise along the stunning coastline which Antony is said to have given Cleopatra as a wedding gift. Later, relax at the breathtaking inlet sheltering the Sunken Baths of Cleopatra.

"Light in nature creates the movement of color."

-Robert Delaunay

THE DYNAMICS OF COLOR
Color Psychology

GREEN
Natural Nurturer

Rebirth, renewal eternal spring
Perpetual growth and health we sing

Praise to Nature's mantle of green
Delicate fern, forest groves serene

Harmonious mix of blue and yellow
Comfortable relaxed and mellow

Feel good; walk on the lush grass
A velvety carpet soothes every lass

Energy rises in a springtime wood
Feeling young, life is understood

Color of abundance brings us cash
So as we give we receive at last

Great givers of love and affection
Compassionate green is the connection

Rejuvenate senses, calm the mind
Peacemaker green is very kind

A relaxing bath in nature's hue
Immerse yourself and renew.

Chapter 6
THE DYNAMICS OF COLOR
Color Psychology

GREEN
Natural Nurturer

Mother Earth's favorite color must have been green as she planted the world in the fresh, vital colors of an eternal spring: a verdant green field, a breezy, billowy meadow, a velvet carpet of moss on the forest floor and trees, which produce chlorophyll, the very life force that purifies the air we breathe.

Faber Birren said, "Like green and you probably dwell in the forest of humanity: you are a respected neighbor, voter, home builder, patronizer and joiner." As such green evokes thoughts of the great forest of humanity where the heart center, the Green Chakra opens up with sympathy, compassion and unconditional love.

Green is balanced with elements of harmony and peacefulness that calms the mind and rejuvenates the senses. As such, the soothing green ray gives a feeling of stability and attracts many people because they feel comfortable in its sustainable orbit.

People who gravitate to green are the nurturers and peacemakers creating harmony in circles of socialization. They are usually smart and resourceful and have problem-solving minds that handle family or business negotiations with diplomacy by creating an atmosphere of cooperation, which encourages everyone to calmly agree to make the right decision.

Such green people have a high moral sense about doing the right thing and are the center of their household, and they love being around family They also make excellent business managers in the workplace. With their compassionate nature and qualities of unconditional love, forgiveness and selflessness, they count among their ranks those wonderful teachers and nannies, the nurturers of children. Similarly other like-minded individuals often take a career path in medicine as doctors or nurses.

Like blooming flowers green growth also represents abundance and stimulates your financial wisdom. Attracted to the monetary value of green paper money you are the type of person who saves and has a hefty bank account. Money and investment opportunities usually come your way and you deal with them with a sound mind. Before making a decision you consider the pros and cons of the offer.

HISTORY: Every great phenomenon has its origin. In Fruhling (Spring) "Vier letzte Lieder" (Four Last Songs, 1948) by the German composer, Richard Strauss (1864-1949), his music evokes dreams of springtime, with its trees, blue skies, and birdsong, and then sees it unfold in all its beauty. This song says it all about how we envision this joyful season of youthful vigor, radiant energy and fresh optimism, and its link to nature, the planet earth and peace.

The word "green" has the universal appeal of nature and comes from the same root as "grow. In its most natural draw it represents a subconscious longing for Spring, the season of re-birth, regeneration and the sustainability and renewal of life.

Green registers as a secondary color, the perfect blending of blue and yellow pigments. Pleasing to the eye, it is the color of most grasses and leaves while growing, of some fruits while they are ripening and the very sea itself. Green is considered a cool color in terms of temperature and is the most balanced of all the color groups.

THE GREEN MOVEMENT: The color green is "Now," the pinnacle color. Ecological concerns have made green a popular color with individuals, corporations, advertising and marketing firms adapting the green mantra in preservation and environmental programs.

The business community has accepted global warming as a fact and is seeking innovations to clean up their supply chains and products. The ranks of Eco-conscious consumers are growing and adults are adopting various Eco-driven behaviors. The (gradual) greening of America has therefore altered consumer attitudes toward products and consumer awareness has resulted in more environmentally friendly goods in the marketplace.

Going Green is also the key to the "sell" and marketing of textiles and companies have taken up the challenge, responding by creating organic cottons that do not use synthetic chemical fertilizers and pesticides during cultivation. A significant growth area is the use of organic cotton baby wear by mothers who want to avoid the presence of harmful pesticides next to their baby's delicate skin.

Consumers have demanded "Organic," natural, healthy food and the green grocers have introduced organic sections in their markets. As consumers became more and more aware of the benefits of eating healthy and protecting their home new food outlets fueled the competition for everything organic. No wonder a produce supplier with the delivery of organic foods and products, has gained in popularity. Shoppers are also favoring open air green markets and rather than "take out" there is a return to cooking meals from scratch with fresh ingredients produced in local farms.

Color takes "bloom" in veggies like brussels sprouts, broccoli, spinach, asparagus, artichoke, zucchini, peas, avocado, green peppers, okra, and salad greens, watercress, chicory, endive and parsley. Herbs like sage, thyme, mint and chives enter the color vocabulary, as does olive, pistachio and lime.

Everyone seems to want to get into the green movement. The color is so prominent that marketing campaigns are sprouting green messages in the headlines of editorials and advertising in newspapers and magazines.

For example, to draw readers attention to a fashion editorial, the word "Paris" in bold black letters appears against a lime green background.

Things you can do: At grocery stores bring a canvas tote in place of paper and plastic shopping bags. Buy products packaged in recyclable materials, avoid items with "too much" plastic packaging and shop in stores that indicate that they're making sustainability a priority.

GREEN REFERENCES: It is interesting to note that since the 1893 American Universities have recognized by code or custom major faculties in which green represents medicine. So green has come full circle, and as pointed out earlier, it is not uncommon today to see surgeons and medical professionals wearing green or blue-green uniforms, especially in operating rooms where the unpleasant glare of white could no longer be tolerated.

Although green has more positive vibes than negative ones green can also represent a person who is referred to as being "green," not quite ripened with maturity. Such a person may appear to lack training or experience and is an easy target to be duped or deceived. Because of their immaturity they often tend to have a jealous streak and may appear to be envious without founded reason.

Thinking of the green's jealous streak, I recall a popular television sitcom, where women, who are "Green with Envy" and have the gift of the gab to keep rumors circulating.

HISTORY: Throughout history, green has been associated with youthful exploration. In ancient Egypt, the ancient god Osiris painted himself with the "wholesome offering" of two bags of green pigment, perhaps to prolong his youth or induce balance and harmony into his life. Green is the special hue of the great Prophet Mohammad and today it is present in the flags of every Muslim country.

Many green associated words have entered the popular color vocabulary. Fashionable Art Deco jade jewelry comes to mind, as does "midori" (green) which the Japanese view as the color of eternal life. Then, too, there are the American Colonial greens of Williamsburg, Virginia and the lovely Celedon Green ceramics of Chinese porcelain.

Before the Great Depression of the 1930s, upbeat green automobiles were popular, but black quickly replaced green as a somber nation faced shortages and economic downturn. Then after WWII the 1950s ushered in another love affair with light and dark greens, which psychologically reflected the nation's desire to bring back harmony and growth in the economy. Yet, today the "Greening of America" has more to do with health and environmental issues than anything else. As the nation strives to establish harmony and balance, Green Peace says it all.

FASHION: A green personality loves to share her fashion ideas because she opens her heart with compassion and outward confidence to make the right color choices. Wearing green says you're a confident fashionista, a woman who appears self-assured and professional.

This rich hue, whether lime, spruce, hunter, shamrock or emerald reflects glowing health and a desire to in harmony with nature. Like fresh, leafy growth bright juicy greens suggest newness and excitement while darker shades can be dramatic and sophisticated. Once considered an anti-fashion, the color green has come full circle in fashion collections. Worn by stars of stage and screen green has been given new status for day and evening wear.

A dark hunter-green tailored wool suit with a matching silk paisley blouse is an office classic that says you're cool, collected and ready to get the job done. You're the kind of individual who can balance your business and personal life with steady confidence. Let the jacket double for weekends and wear it with a soft melon-orange cashmere sweater and denim jeans for a casual look.

It's rare to see a professional man wearing a green business suit, but there is an exception. Men look classic and sharp on the weekend wearing a hunter-green sports jacket with a beige turtleneck and beige denim jeans.

A woman wearing a spruce-green tweed wool coat, fashioned with an over-sized wing collar and asymmetrical button closure, lets everyone know she is a trendsetter.

Knee-length cocktail dresses have all the luck of the Irish in lime green satin. Such an "on trend" dress makes an eye-catching entrance and looks positively "Wow" on young women.

Other dresses go out on the the town eyed by spectators "green with envy." For instance, a form-fitting spearmint green taffeta party shift with a plunging neckline provides all the glamour one needs to wear on a beautiful spring night. In another take, dazzling jewel-colored emerald green hits the curves in an hourglass cocktail dress.

You'll be every bit a green angel in a strapless evening gown in multi-layered green tones of silk chiffon that creates the perfect palette for a dramatic evening of dancing. With a confidant smile choose a rich emerald green plush-velvet evening suit and sweep into any social occasion as if you were the Queen of the Forest.

HOME FURNISHINGS: As people seek to bring the beauty of nature into their home environments, the color green becomes more and more appealing because of its sense of balance and normalcy. When you enter a home where there are plants or a green themed décor, it conjures a feeling of warmth and welcome, because the color has a way of signaling acceptance and hospitality. In such color scheme you feel nurtured and relaxed.

Nature's go-with-everything color brings the outdoors into the living room in the subtle shade of "Fern," a fresh tint that is stabilizing and serene. A leafy green sofa catches the beams of sunlight that dance around the room. While pale celery green toss pillows imprinted with large green ferns convey nature's invitation to relax in the comfort of its bounty. Think eucalyptus, evergreen boughs, holly branches, ferns and other rubber plants to create an indoor garden.

For a long time green has had a negative reputation. It has been in and out of the decorator's vocabulary. I remember seeing pictures of my mother's avocado green kitchen and bathroom of the 1950's. Back then, avocado was considered the height of interior decorating status but it fell out of favor.

However, today shades and tints of green have had comeback interest, perhaps encouraged by the Eco-friendly green movement.

You can connect your kitchen with nature by the magic of painting the walls in a pale, sun-kissed green. The color creates a harmonious ambiance that centers your workload with balance and helps to give you a "can do" attitude.

Go the the craft store to find décor ideas. For example, to introduce the ivy theme purchase green vine wall appliques and past them around a bare kitchen window, then add miniature bird cages at the top corners of the window.

If you want to incorporate a touch of green elsewhere shop for counter top accessories like a toaster, a tension taming green tea kettle, a skid proof slicing board in bright lime or purchase vibrant green cookware.

PRODUCTS: In the green age movement, the enthusiasm for more environmentally friendly products are hitting the shelves from cosmetics and fragrances, to fashion, home furnishings to automobiles. The cosmetics industry is taking the green movement more seriously and has a huge stake in green products.

Since color is basically what the beauty industry is selling going green also means eliminating excessive packaging. For example, St. Ives Elements advertises green packaging for an "Olive Cleanser" and "Olive Scrub. Then there's Yves Saint Laurent's Color Harmony for eyes in the "Garden of Eden" collection and in Jergens' Naturals "Refresh" moisturizer says it all with a green leaf packaging design.

The perfume industry has also embraced the green movement with packaging and fragrances that appeal to our emotions. Shiseido's perfume, for example, calls on our senses, advertising its perfume, "Zen," as the fragrance, the sensation, the emotion. Aromas tell another story and appeal to our sense of smell. Think marjoram, rose oil, yarrow and orris root.

Chic fashions in fabrics made of soy, hemp and other organic materials say you're part of the green movement. In the book "Gorgeously Green," every girl's guide to an earth-friendly life, Sophie Uliano, offers Eco-friendly tips that make it fun to shop.

Dish washing liquid made from plants provide a natural way to make dishes spanking clean. And it is easy to stop trashing the environment with Go Green garbage bags. Green labeling says "non-toxic" in an environmentally-friendly formula in a stain and odor eliminator household product.

Green spas boast Eco-friendly environments where you slip into a bamboo robe and unwind in a green sanctuary where huge overhead skylights allow natural light to filter into the planted green oasis. Beauty practitioners give organic facials and body treatments using an allover green exfoliator and cucumber face mask.

CHAKRA: The Green Chakra (the heart). This healing hue is associated with the thymus gland. It connects you to nature and relates to the health of your heart, lungs, chest area, upper back and hands.

By visualizing the green ray of harmony, love and empathy you can call upon our true compassionate and open-hearted nature. Brotherhood and sympathy will become your mantra. Like the great forest of humanity, green acts in the rebirth and renewal of your body, mind and spirit. It restores hope and banishes indecision.

You are are a compassionate care-giver and love taking care of others. That is why family is the center of your life and cherished friends benefit from your loyal, loving friendship.

Meditating on the Green Chakra encourages love and a balanced lifestyle. It also represents unconditional love, the kind of love that a mother gives to her children by encouraging their dreams and aspirations.

Pets, particularly dogs, are in the green orbit as they give unconditional love sometimes with extraordinary consequences. This calls to mind the loyalty of a dog in the classic Scottish tale, Greyfriar's Bobby, about a Skye terrier who lived in 19th century Edinburgh, England. This faithful little dog, in the classic tale, spent fourteen years guarding his master's grave until his own death January 14, 1872. A book, Greyfriar's Bobby (1912) by Eleanor Atkinson, and a movie were also inspired by the little dogs loyalty.

MUSIC: Upon listening to a recent concert I was inspired to write the following: "Music is a highly personal experience. It transports us to memories, to inner reflections on happy times, to love and to sadness. Suspended in moments of reverie we escape the mundane and we are elevated to realms of poetic beauty far beyond one's ordinary imagination." There is much debate among music scholars as to the validity about the relationship between music and color.

Sir Isaac Newton, in his day, probably in deference to the seven notes of the diatonic music scale to the seven spheres identified by the early astronomers drew this conclusion. He chose seven colors for the musical scale giving the musical note F for the color green.

Further evidence of the relationship between color and music concerns some pop singers, who has a neurological condition known as sound-to-color synesthesia. When they hear certain notes and sounds corresponding colors appear.

Sometimes music can convey nature in an uplifting orchestration. Hal A. Lingerman in the book, "The Healing Energies of Music" wrote, "I like beautiful melodies of the Italian Baroque composer, Antonio Vivaldi (1678-1741). In the Four Seasons, Concerto No. 1 'Spring,' in the Largo they are effervescent, flowing like a stream. The text tells how the goat herder sleeps with his trusty dog beside him; the languorous musical setting is interrupted only by the 'barking' of a solo viola."

Vivaldi"s music is usually happy, uncomplicated, warm and genial. At times you can hear imitations of nature songs and bird calls. When you listen to Vivaldi's The Four Seasons, Op 8, including Summer, Autumn and Winter, it takes you back to nature in all its splendor. In the text, evoked in this famous musical masterpiece, the melodies soothe and relax.

EAT YOUR GREENS: Fruits and veggies have a rainbow connection and the more colors that come together in a meal the better the nutrition. Broccoli may not be your favorite food but it is one of the healthiest, so is spinach. Broccoli is a detoxinator, a powerful, natural antibiotic, a cancer fighter that contains vitamins A, C and K. Cooks beware: Don't let broccoli get mushy and lose its nutrients, it is best steamed al dente. Guacamole may be a tasty treat but instead consider eating plain avocado, which is packed with heart smart nutrients.

Are your nerves frazzled? According to Penn State scientist Sheila G. West, Ph.D, popping pistachios every day for a month can significantly reduce the effects of everyday stress and tension. Why? The high levels of unsaturated fats and antioxidants improve circulation so that blood pressure doesn't spike even during anxious moments. There's nothing common about parsley. It is rich and uncommonly high in Vitamin C, which increases the body's supply of anti-cold proteins. One of the most reasonably priced veggies, parsley adds nutrients to sauces, soups, salads and sandwiches.

DRINK GREEN TEA: Volumes have been written about the benefits of drinking Green Tea and green tea blends that promise health, beautification and longevity. Why? Green tea has plenty of fat-burning antioxidants, it protects your liver from cancer, lowers cholesterol and fights heart disease. It sounds like a magic cure all, but regular drinking green tea is an inexpensive way to improve mind, body and spirit.

Beauty consultants tell me that you can also zap dandruff and relieve an itchy scalp with a green tea rinse. Brew two tea bags, let cool and then massage into your scalp and hair daily for three days. For complete benefits it is best to do the treatment on a weekend when you can let the rinse stay in overnight.

TRIVIA: Have ya got any Greenbacks? That's slang for a dollar bill in United States currency. And if you're a newcomer to this country or an inexperienced person you're called a Greenhorn. Obviously, you will need a Green Card, a U.S. permit for aliens allowing residence and employment.

If you have adapted organic, then develop a Green Thumb, the ability to successful grow plants or veggies. Then, too, you may need a Greenhouse, a sunny glass enclosed structure to cultivate your plantings that the Green Grocer will eventually purchase in the farmer's market.

No space for a Greenhouse? Well, do what the women did during WWII and create a Victory Garden to grow your veggies right in your own backyard. Not even a patch of earth? Then grow your stuff in a window box just like those practical women did to supplement the food shortages.

Romantic English poet, John Keats (1795-1821) captured the essence of green in his poem, 'Endymion':

"Fill your baskets high
With fennel green and golden pines,
Savory latter-mint and columbines,
Cool parsley basil sweet and sunny thyme,
Yea, every flower and leaf of every clime
All gathered in the dewy morning."

Take the Green Light, is the "Go" signal to cross the street or to proceed with a project or course of action. However, let's avert the Greenhouse Effect the possibility of the atmospheric heating phenomenon.

The Green Room, however, in a theater, concert hall or TV studio is a privileged place for performers when off-stage.

Born in May your birthstone is Emerald, known as the Queen of Gems and the gem of queens. You may not be a 'Royal,' but wearing the stone suggests a regal bearing and social personality. Most green individuals are great conversationalists because emeralds claim to grant you the gift of eloquence.

Emerald's unique range of green tones, from the light-hardheartedness of pale to deep rich shades, are especially soothing. The ancients held emerald in great esteem, believing it would sharpened the wearer's eyesight and mind. Other green related gemstones include tourmaline, green jade, and quartz. Then, too, Sardinia, Italy lays claim to the Emerald Coast.

Imbibing green has a sinister history. Paris in a bygone era was converged upon by artists, the intellectuals and performers not only for its artistic liberalism, but also for its the famed "l'heure vert," (the green hour) where at cafes on the Rive Gauche (Left Bank) they drank "Absinthe," the fabled, ghastly greenish liquor. It was imbibed with such gusto and drunkenness that it was almost banned from café life.

However, on the positive side it stimulated the minds of the art intelligentsia. It is no wonder, therefore, that absinthe induced creativity crept into the canvases of such French painters as the famed impressionist, Edouard Manet (1832-83). His painting "The Absinthe Philosopher," 1859 depicts the decadence and the pathos of the era.

Let's not forget the Green Mountain Boys. During the American Revolution these soldiers from Vermont , originally organized by Ethan Allen around 1770, opposed the territorial claims of New York. Then, too, today we remember the Green Beret soldiers, symbolic of their enlistment in the U.S. Army Special forces.

Born in August your birthstone is peridot, a vivid green gemstone with just a hint of gold that compliments a fresh, light summer wardrobe. It is the gemstone choice of a balanced personality that keeps nerves cool and in control. The stone is so ancient that it can be found in Egyptian jewelry as early as the 2nd millennium B.C.

Memories, memories, I just love remembering the English colorist and author, Kate Greenaway (1846-1901) and her exquisite books "A Day in a Child's Life" (1881) and "Under the Window" (1879). Such treasures are as wonderful to read today as they were long ago. And who can forget the endearing image of Babar, the whimsical elephant dressed in a green suit and wearing a yellow crown, that became an all-time favorite with generations of readers?

French illustrator and storyteller, Jean de Brunhoff (1899-1937), created the first book, "Histoire de Babar, le petit elephant" (l93l). Years later his son, Laurent de Brunhoff, (b. 1925) continued the enduring fictional world with "Babar et ce coquin d'Arthur" (1946).

Then there's the luck of the Irish and the wearing of the green on St. Patrick's Day. In folklore we hear of green fairies with green eyes, green hair and even green skin, which calls to mind the musical Brigadoon, (1947), book and Lyrics by Alan J. Lerner and music by Frederick Loewe in which Leprechaun characters from a fairy world play a pivotal role in the story. It is said that if humans want to see the falries, all they have to do is put a four-leaf clover in a hat, and the magic begins.

"Ti's Yourself" who is welcomed in by the fairy shamrock of Irish hospitality, and to hear the wit of the Irish listen to the gift of the Blarney that only the wee folk can dish out. Perhaps the Leprechauns, being the true spirit of Ireland, will help us find that pot of gold at the end of the rainbow.

There's so much that is good about green. We embrace its bounty every day with imagery of lush green fields that restore health and peaceful contemplation of all things beautiful in nature. "To One in Paradise," a poem by America's own, Edgar Allan Poe (1809-49), sums it up this way:

> *Thou wast all that to me, love,*
> *For which my soul did pine--*
> *A green isle in the sea, love,*
> *A fountain and a shrine,*
> *All wreathed with fairy fruits and flowers,*
> *And all the flowers were mine.*

THE DYNAMICS OF COLOR
Color Psychology

CHARTREUSE
A Sassy Color

Fresh as spring, acidic and pert
Chartreuse vibrations keep alert

A festive mood, effervescent, too
Yellow and green, this sassy hue

Lives up to its snappy reputation
Whimsicality and a fun sensation

Enlarge spaciousness in chartreuse
Paint a room and increase your muse

A festive color sparks neon-green
Changes like a chameleon to preen

Bite of citrus, limeade pleasures
Festive Chartreuse is the measure

Libations divine in chartreuse time
Celebrations straight from the vine

Of feminine fashions on review
Chartreuse begs for a twirl or two

Candy dish mints an Easter egg cue
Dip into the pot of this happy hue.

Chapter 7
THE DYNAMICS OF COLOR
Color Psychology

CHARTREUSE
A Sassy Color

Chartreuse by any other name would not be so ambiguous. It is a color halfway between green and yellow on the color wheel and as such is 50% green and 50% yellow. This equality has substantial benefits providing the balance and harmony of green with the happy and innate wisdom of yellow.

Chartreuse is a color that has status in some circles and is loathed in others. Painters, for example, have often used the shock value of chartreuse to snap our attention. For example, French painter, Henri Matisse (1869-1954) used color as the primary source of pictorial drama. In 1905 he painted, "The Green Line," a portrait of his wife with a startling chartreuse line running vertically on her face. Matisse stated that he wished to render the emotion that a subject evoked in him, rather then depict its literal appearance.

Pulling up the ranks to modern times, American artist, Mary Heilmann puts a jolt of the chartreuse in her color saturated abstraction, and simply calls it Chartreuse (1987).

Chartreuse was named because of its resemblance to the green color of one of the French liqueurs called green Chartreuse and another equally potent version, which was made later called yellow Chartreuse. Chartreuse runs the whole color gamut from bright to acidly green-yellow varieties that crop up in fashion as well as industrial products.

Since 1973, for example, a sort of fluorescent chartreuse, more yellow than green, has been adopted as the color of fire engines in parts of the United States and elsewhere. The reason behind this is that chartreuse fire engines are more visible on the streets than traditional red fire engines. In Australia and New Zealand this form of chartreuse yellow is also known as "Act Yellow."

PERSONALITY: If you gravitate towards chartreuse you are a person who not only lives the in great forest of humanity but you have the wisdom to live abundantly as well. Chartreuse is a brilliant and happy hue. Chose it and you can be counted on to have a sunshine personality that enables everyone to look on the bright side of any situation and feel happy about it.

You're a good organizer and people respect your ability to influence everyone to cooperate and arrive at sensible solutions.

The Chartreuse personality can sometimes appear rather haughty, but that is only because they are so high minded. You might find that such a person works in academia, is a librarian administrator or becomes an antiquarian, lover of books. However, that does not mean that they a bookish and boring. On the contrary, Chartreuse people are gregarious at heart and they happily share their knowledge with those people who indicate interest. Chartreuse individuals love to bask in the limelight and a little flattery will encourage their dissertation.

HISTORY: The Order of Chartreuse was more than 500 years old when, in 1605, at a Chartreuse monastery in Vauvet, a small suburb of Paris, Francois Hannibal d'Estrees gave the Chartreuse, aka Carthusian monks, an already ancient and treasured manuscript entitled, "An Elixir of Long Life." It's original intent was for use as a tonic, a health remedy.

However, in the 17th century only a few monks and even fewer apothecaries understood the use of herbs and plants in the treatment of illness. The manuscript's recipe was so complex that only bits and pieces of it were understood.

Nonetheless, the recipe was unraveled far from Paris at the Order of Chartreuse, a Catholic monastery, in the mother house of the Cartesian monks, located high in the rugged mountains just north of Grenoble, France. There apothecary, Frere Jerome Maubec, finally succeeded in unraveling the complexities of the recipe and Chartreuse Elixir was created.

At that time the potion was considered a cure all for illness not as an aperitif as it is known today. Today this "Elixir of Long Life" is still made and sold exclusively by Chartreuse monks following that ancient recipe, and is called Elixir Vegetal de la Grande Chartreuse (Herbal Elixir). It is reputed to be a very effective tonic, and it was intended to preserve health and prolong life.

THE BEVERAGE: This "liqueur of health" follows an ancient, but potent secret formula of 130 natural plants, herbs and other botanicals macerated in alcohol. It was so tasty that its role changed from advocating health benefits to that of a beverage rather than a medicine.

In 1764 the monks adapted the elixir recipe to make a milder beverage which we know today as Chartreuse Verde (Green Chartreuse) liqueur 110 proof. And in 1838 they introduced an even milder concoction called Chartreuse Jaune (Yellow Chartreuse) 80 proof.

Today only two monks have been entrusted by the Order with the secret of producing these liqueurs and only these two know the correct combination of plants and flowers that yield the green or yellow colors. The sale of the liqueurs based on the already-ancient manuscript of 1605 allows the Chartreuse monks the funds necessary to dedicate their lives to prayer and meditation.

The ancient stone corridors of the monastery, the cellar and distillery are lined with enormous barrels of the precious liquid. To visit the Chartreuse Cellars consult: the Musee de La Grande Chartreuse: www.musee-grande-chartreuse.fr.

FASHION: Chartreuse is a color name that often crops up when the fashionistas describe fashion. It is an ambiguous color because Chartreuse can mean green or it can mean yellow just like the liqueur Chartreuse, which comes in both colors. Then too, there is the color called, Yellow-Green, which shares complementary Chartreuse characteristics.

When it comes to fashion there's always some variation of Chartreuse green that makes a comeback in spring. It's renewal time and green reflects our need to be in harmony with nature. The yellow component has familiar overtones of a sunny disposition with a hint of warmth in a snappy, happy persona that projects a perky youthful appearance.

When worn alone, Yellow-Green brings a fresh appearance to any outfit. Depending on its intensity it can have neon brightness that lights up a winter coat with eye-popping drama. Yellow-Green Chartreuse also translates eye popping drama in a business blazer with bold over-sized buttons.

Yellowy Chartreuse, however, can appear acidic and such a jacket looks best when toned down with a navy pencil slim skirt or worn with black pants for a more sophisticated career look. A chartreuse paisley wool Pashmina tossed over a shapely sleeveless purple dress makes a striking statement that says you're a style innovator and a smart dresser.

The deeper, more intense yellow-green moves into the night in darker moss green tones that reflect the moonlight in a chameleon affect. When you're wearing a lush velvet strapless evening gown the light of candles or chandeliers changes moss green from light to dark depending on where you are on the dance floor. Such a look conveys the message that you are an elegant and a sophisticated partner.

Iridescent, lemony-green taffeta tells another chameleon story in a satin cocktail dress. Shimmering with the ballroom lights you project the youthful persona of a happy party girl.

HOME FURNISHINGS: In home décor the ambiguity of yellow-green Chartreuse makes it a compromising color. Yet, furnishings half green and half yellow, like the content of the Chartreuse liqueur, can still make a statement.

The wall of a home or office, for example, painted in soft translucent green, has more livable appeal and creates a clear, clean background for modern chrome furniture. In spaces like hallways where people merely pass through, light yellow-green Chartreuse can enliven the area twofold. You get a burst of sunshine from yellow and green lets you take the stairs with balance and youthful vigor. Add lush green bamboo plants and the area takes on zen-like quiet and promotes a peaceful walk through for individuals who enter this green glen.

A new trend in functional furniture for dens, home offices or corporate settings comes from firms that puts color into the workplace with eye-popping results. File cabinets, go-cart desks and coffee tables in off-shoot colors from chartreuse such as 'fresh new twist of lime peel' or 'key lime pie' have sunny overtones with the benefit of leafy green harmony. This yellow-green equipment gives a new meaning to functional décor.

In rooms with white-washed-walls, green revolutionizes how color can perk up the office worker with positive vibes. Green, in this instance, promotes a healthy outlook as well as revitalizing energy.

When kitchen cabinets need a face lift think chartreuse to let sunshine into the dining area where just a hint of green brings nature's bounty into the home environment. The effect of a warm green décor creates a festive, entertaining mood and makes any kitchen the center of harmonious family gatherings.

TRIVIA: In Quentin Tarantino's book, "Death Proof," the bar owner Warren (Quentin Tarantino) serves a green liqueur. After having emptied their glasses, and being asked what was served, Warren says, "Chartreuse, the only liqueur so good they named a color after it."

Chartreuse comes up here and there in other stories. In John Updike's short story "Domestic Life in America," first published in the New Yorker and later in the short story collection *Problems, Jean* offers her separated husband Fraser a libation, some Chartreuse, as they go over her proposed alimony budget.

Fraser asks: "Where does the money for Chartreuse come in?" Jean replies: "Under 'household necessities.'"

Then in F. Scott Fitzgerald's novel *The Great Gatsby*, Gatsby shares a bottle of Chartreuse with Nick, the narrator in Chapter Five:

"Finally we came to Gatsby's own apartment, a bedroom and a bath, and an Adam study, where we sat down and drank a glass of some Chartreuse he took from a cupboard in the wall."

My Canadian grandmother must have known something about the legendary use of Chartreuse as a health remedy. Based on an ancient recipe, that she claims she received from a monk, my grandmother would make a bottle of Chartreuse each spring by placing a variety of herbs in alcohol. Then the bottle was left secured in a cupboard to macerate for a year.

In the cold Canadian winters the resulting yellow-green Chartreuse liqueur was a welcoming treat that warmed our spirits, even a wee dram for the young ones.

In literature there is a book called, 'The Girl from the Chartreuse' by Pierre Peju, and also the title of the adapted film by Jean-Pierre Denise. Going back to the 19th century the famous French writer Stendhal wrote 'La Chartreuse de Parme' (English: The Charterhouse of Parma).

What could be more fitting as a tribute to the yellowish-green Chartreuse than the perfumed water created and given by a Chartreuse monk to Wilhelm Mulhens as a gift for his marriage. It is known today as "4711 Eau de Cologne."

As for longevity the "Elixir of Long Life," Chartreuse may indeed be one of the world's oldest concoctions for it certainly has an ancient history going back to the 1600s. Let's hope, therefore, that with its legend of prolonging a long life, that the color Chartreuse will rejuvenate your mind and body and awaken your spirit to embrace life in a brand new way.

Chapter 8
THE DYNAMICS OF COLOR
Color Psychology

YELLOW
Joyful Sunshine

Kissed by the sun
Yellow is for everyone

An eternal summer's day
Welcome sunshine we pray

A Cheerful, joyful hue
Brings happy smiles anew

Yellow's high on visibility
Shiny slicker sensibility

Even if it showers
Think of yellow flowers

Mellow 'n youthful
Yellow is so fruitful

Dollops of Yellow soothes
Cheers those who brood

Bask in sunshine rays
To yellow we give praise

For a sunny disposition
Put gloom in remission

Get your attitude glowing
Energize your knowing

Tarty, tangy uplifting
Creativity is re-sifting

Take a brisk lemon twist
Start the day with a kiss

Chapter 8
THE DYNAMICS OF COLOR
Color Psychology

Yellow
Joyful Sunshine

Sunshine, sunflowers, a yellow umbrella on a rainy day, a cheerful disposition, intellectual pursuits, brainy decisions make the second primary color, yellow, the happiest color in the spectrum. It's color temperature is the warmth of a summer-perfect day, inspired by the health-generating rays of the sun.

Yellow represents a sunny, upbeat, optimistic and enthusiastic disposition. If you opt for sunshine yellow, you are naturally a warm-hearted, kind and considerate person who takes time to be considerate, compassionate and sympathetic. You're the sunshine in everyone's life and that is why people flock to the positive vibes cast out by your sunny personality.

Without sunshine the world would certainly be a depressing place. Yellow is a color that livens up an individual's mood with cheerfulness, hope and youthful expectations. No wonder those buttons and stickers with a smiley face against a yellow background say, "Have a Good Day."

Yellow is the color of hope and optimism. So it is fitting that Tony Orlando's song, "Tie a Yellow Ribbon Round the Old Oak Tree," is symbolic of the tying of yellow ribbons on trees and buildings. It helps us to remember the troops overseas and we keep the ribbons up until they come home to remind us "mission accomplished."

However, the legend of the yellow ribbon goes deeper, back to 1876, when the ribbon symbolized the struggle for women's rights.

The sunshine ray attracts people who have the "smarts." If you identify with yellow, the symbol of knowledge and clarity, it's because you are an intellectually minded individual who has a shrewd personality. Your mental clarity makes you a logical and precise thinker, and with these attributes, on or off the job, you are usually an organized decision-maker.

However, you balance your yellow personality with a strong sense of humor, which usually attracts people to join your circle of friends. Pick yellow and it will say that you are a cheerful, energetic person whose joy and optimism are spontaneous.

You're the one who bolsters up everyone else to see the bright side of any situation. Yellow is all about career success. It is the power color in ties worn by executive hopefuls on Wall street. And, have you noticed, it is the color of legal pads and business documents?

Yellow, however, like all the other colors, has a positive-negative relationship. As a matter of fact, yellow sometimes even has a bad reputation. The negative side of yellow depends on its application. Statements like "yellow bellied," or "yellow dog" remind us of cowardice and treason.

Greenish-yellow reminds us of illness and an overdose of yellow can heighten temper tantrums, even cause depression. This calls to mind, the mesmerizing 1892 fiction novel, "The Yellow Wallpaper," by Charlotte Perkins Gilman (1860-1935). The play, inspired by the book, was produced by the Manhattan School of Music (New York City).

Primarily the depressed female character tears down the wallpaper in a claustrophobic single room. There she has been confined by her physician husband for an undisclosed condition, and she eventually goes mad. This example of one of the most negative reactions to a yellow environment is extreme, but it does provide compelling evidence that the color can have dramatic consequences.

In its finest interpretation, yellow speaks of happiness and individuals who prefer this color radiate positive sparkle. They combine many positive traits, at once whimsical, sunny, cheerful, friendly and they bring sunshine and fun times into our lives. Pick yellow and you will project an outgoing, energetic and radiant personality that is never at a loss for friends.

Yellow reminds us of our favorite images: a yellow taxicab, a yellow school bus. Fruits call to mind bananas, lemons pineapples, grapefruit and golden delicious apples, and veggies, like yams, yellow peppers and parsnips. Daffodils make us think of spring and sunflowers make us smile.

FASHION: Yellow has multiple meanings and fashion color cards conjure up a myriad of names to describe yellow. Easter is yellow and so is spring. In summer it puts you in child-like mood of joyful playfulness, the yearning for freedom and youthful aspirations. In the flower world, dwell your yellow thoughts on daisies, sunflowers, yellow tulips and daffodils.

For tempting treats conjure up, remember, delicious lemonade, lemon drops, lemon tarts, lemon ices, pineapple or grapefruit. Remember summer classics like yellow rain slickers, sunshine, suntans and sun bathing.

Blonde Renaissance beauties were idealized in paintings and poetry, and if "Gentlemen Prefer Blondes," its far easier to dip into the bottle and go blonde all the way. For a touch of glamour blonde hair highlights brighten the complexion and candlelight heightens romance in the night.

There are many ways to wear yellow and recharge your fashion image. Yellow lets everyone know that you are outgoing, confident and highly motivated. A classic marigold yellow, single breasted jacket worn with a crisp white blouse and a pencil-slim, knee-length black skirt says you're ready to make a sharp decision, but you'll think it over and decide calmly. It tells everyone you are a fair decision-maker. Wear the same blazer with cigarette-slim black pants on the weekend and the look is eye-popping chic and you're ready for fun.

Fashionable outfits in other spectrum colors can benefit from perky yellow. A royal blue suit worn with punchy yellow pumps turns on the drama as do accessories like a matching yellow print scarf to brighten your face and a yellow leather satchel to tote your possessions around from day into evening.

VISIBILITY: Since yellow has high visibility a bright yellow trench coat or shiny splash boots are wardrobe essentials, and a bright yellow umbrella on a rainy day creates a sunshine glow overhead. Active wear and separates make an energetic statement in bright yellow and when combined with reds, greens or navy, it brings attention to the wearer as a self-assured contender in the world of sports. To boost confidence and visibility wear yellow with black. For weekend fashionistas radiant yellow jeans highlight your legs with weekend style.

Yellow is a pick-me-up color and whenever you wear it yellow can put you in a snappy, happy mood. By night yellow becomes a chameleon and can make you feel dynamic or mellow. When yellow appears in sumptuous satin, silks, taffeta or velvet it assumes a more dramatic role that suggests movie star quality, a person who is not afraid to flaunt her femininity.

Fashion designers have come up with a parade of hot-to-trot chrome-yellow party dresses.

Youthful above the knee length styles range from the flirtatious strapless cocktail dress to asymmetric off-the-shoulder dinner gowns. Then, too, form-fitting sheath dresses with sarong wrapped skirts let you party on through the night with a gay, sunny disposition.

A soft creamy yellow silk chiffon asymmetric evening gown with cascading ruffles might well take its inspiration from the colors of the Florentine Renaissance painter, "Sandro" Botticelli (1444-1510) and reflect your enlightened creativity. While a sheer organza dance dress, with a full skirt, in layer gradations from pale to vivid yellow, conveys the subtle impression that you dance with youthful abandon, and are the 'life of the party.'

UTILITARIAN: Considering yellow's high visibility wavelengths it is no wonder that fluorescent yellow has been adapted for uniforms and protective gear worn by fire fighters, seamen and public utility workers and bicyclists for safety purposes, and because it makes them more visible through smog, dense smoke and fog. Similarly in most parts of the United States and elsewhere fire trucks and utility vehicles are also painted fluorescent yellow because they are more visible on the streets than the traditional red fire engines.

Children's rain wear and splash boots in fluorescent yellow serve the same purpose in providing higher visibility to recognize children crossing the streets. Channeling the same purpose bright yellow "Children at Play" street signs warn motorists to proceed with caution.

Yellow has always been a favorite color for children's wear and juvenile clothing saturated in yellow is a good anecdote to put a smile on a child's face or to brighten their mood on a sullen day. Mothers and teachers can also benefit from the uplifting benefits of yellow. For example, a buttery cream wall soothes and lets sunlight into the room.

HOME FURNISHINGS: Just like sunshine yellow is a warm, welcoming color that can brighten your home and make it cheerful all year. A yellow environment banishes gloom and elicits an upbeat, happy mood. Very few people can be sad in such a sunshine atmosphere.

I love the way the Southerners use the pineapple as a symbol of welcome, placing the motif on garden fences, their porches and even in decorative carvings on four-poster bedroom furniture. The pineapple motif says, "You're most welcome, come again."

Yellow keeps a room looking fresh and new. It invites people to linger longer in such a warm and mellow environment. A yellow kitchen, for example, exudes hospitality in any home and keeps company happily engaged together in lively conversation. The atmosphere is so charged with conviviality, it may even be difficult to get guests to go home.

That is what happened in the yellow dining room, when I visited the historical home of French painter, Claude Monet (1840-1926) in Giverny, France. I remember, we wanted to linger longer in the yellow dining room, which seemingly pulled the light and sunshine into the house just as Monet did in his painting, "Impression: Sunrise"(1872).

BRILLIANT MINDS: The infusion of yellow is also beneficial for serious study because this is the color of wisdom and clarity. People who are drawn to yellow are usually intuitive and intelligent. Yellow intensifies the learning process and stimulates intellectual pursuits. Instead of painting a whole room yellow, you can boost memory simply by using vivid yellow decorative accessories like a lampshade, toss pillows, a yellow bed quilt or just by adding sun-drenched yellow curtains that let inspiration in.

Scandinavian modern furniture, for instance, has pared-down modern style with timeless appeal. When yellow side tables anchor either side of a blue denim couch, the jolt of yellow perks up the room and enlivens social activity with lively conversation.

DARK ROOMS: Environmentally yellow is a sunshine booster. It can seemingly bring sunshine into an otherwise lackluster room or space that may lack a window. Such a room's walls painted in a soft banana shade or mellow-like-butter-yellow in a dark area of the home or office, will brighten not only the mind but exude an uplifting feeling in that space.

The benefits of yellow were clearly expressed by the famed Dutch painter, Vincent Van Gogh (1853-90) when he lived in the provincial region of Arles in Provence, France, where he sought sunshine for his health.

In September 1888, Van Gogh corresponded with his sister Willamina about the 'Yellow House' saying, "My house here is painted outside in the yellow of fresh butter, with garish green shutters. Inside I can live, breathe, and think and paint." His thought sums up so well the significance of sunshine to stimulate an individual's environment. Van Gogh wrote these thoughts to his sister who shared the same depressing illness.

Yellow gives any room a warm, inviting and cheery feeling. A yellow ceiling in a child's room, for example, suggests that the beneficial ray of sunlight is always overhead. Students also benefit from a moderate yellow décor, which encourages study and intellectual pursuits.

On the negative side, an entire room painted bright yellow can be over stimulating and studies have shown that this strong intensity can increase nervousness. More serious consequences can also occur because temperamental people tend to explode in a strong yellow environment. Remember Gilman's "The Yellow Wallpaper," mentioned earlier, that's a good example of how an overly saturated yellow room can result in mental depression.

TURN THE HEAT UP: In a cold room in an office or home yellow, a component of the warm side of the color palette, can strike up a balance and warm up the environment. People seemingly feel warmed by the yellow ambiance and their disposition changes to one that is more friendly and cheerful.

In the workplace, it's been proven that when a cool blue-green factory was changed to the warm palette of yellow, red and orange there were less absentees and people were happier and more productive.

Accent colors can also add dimension and interest to a room's yellow color scheme. Chose violet, yellow's complementary color from the opposite side of the color wheel and the effect is young, fresh and very inviting. The combination creates an atmosphere of lighthearted happiness and fosters creative inspiration.

PRODUCTS sold in grocery stores, in yellow packaging, have high visibility because the eye registers most quickly to yellow and that is why you instinctively select that item first. Just consider the consumer draw to the brilliant yellow packaging of Kodak film, the yellow container for Newman's Own lemonade. Then, too, the yellow legal pad or yellow highlighter you choose helps you to remember important details and encourages creative writing.

BEAUTIFICATION The beauty business has gone all out with products that are tuned into the Chakras or suggest new age benefits that offer joyful enlightenment and soaring spirituality. Yellow liquid bath products and body splashes are color-cued to release balance and harmony, and provide day-to-day well being.

Yellow-tinted moisturizers provide hope in a jar for a youthful appearance. While "on-trend" yellow nail polish may help to connect you to your higher self. Anyone who needs brightening up can benefit from yellow in all its various product applications because it vicariously brings in a touch of sunshine and enhances a dynamic personality. Individuals who are in the yellow orbit are body conscious and stay active throughout their life, even if means going to the gym every day.

Alluding to the benefits of yellow, "Look Sharp," says a popular leomon-based drink product, "Pump it Up, Refresh, Replenish and Recharge." On another note, lemon scent is associated with cleanliness and that is why so many cleaning products have a lemon base color to attract consumer spending.

MEDITATION: Color practitioners and therapists advise to meditate on yellow to realize your greatest potential for happiness and the fulfillment of your highest aspirations. As you contemplate the yellow ray it stimulates higher mentality in a haven of sunshine, that opens up awareness to new interests, intellectual pursuits, expansive ideas and enlightened creativity. It is also the color of intellectual enrichment and clear, precise decision making.

There are several techniques to get you into the yellow mood. However, it is important to settle down in a very private and quite place. Some people can merely close their eyes and see yellow, but most of us need something tangible to promote the meditation.

To jump-start the mediation process if you have a sheer yellow chiffon scarf loosely drape it over your head. At first you can see through the chiffon and when your mind has captured the color visually, then proceed to meditate. If a scarf is not available try wearing yellow tinted sunglasses. You can also buy a yellow colored gel sheet at an art supply store. Hold the gel up to the window, look through the gel and let the yellow ray filter through your mind's eye. As you feel the knowledge and wisdom of yellow surround you, think of a particular problem you wish to solve. Meditate on receiving answers.

Choose the goal you wish to achieve and focus on just one thought at a time. For example, intellectual aspirations might be high on your list, but health and love may also enter into your heart's desire.

However, the exact procedure to follow in the meditation process is a highly personal choice. Results are best realized when you learn a meditation technique by attending a class given by an accredited holistic practitioner. Meditation-specific books are also available at the public library, and also sold in new age or holistic retail stores.

ENERGY RECHARGE According to a British study when you want to recharge your concentration simply look outside your window and gaze at the sun. Why? Because sunlight activates areas of the brain responsible for maintaining alertness and helps you to feel clear-headed almost instantly.

The sun is at the center of the life force itself and is essential for all around good health. Foremost the sun produces vitamin D, which protects against weak bones and supports a healthy heart.

EAT YOUR COLORS: There's a tapestry of lush yellow foods to enrich your palate. However, healthy eating means wisely choosing a spectrum of colorful fruits or vegetables.

When it comes to yellow think yellow bell peppers, yellow turnips and yellow corn which are rich in vitamin A and contain Carotenoids, an antioxidant that helps protect against cancer and damage caused by light and oxygen. Mellow yellow, low fat Swiss cheese and the yellow yolk of an egg also provide good nutrition as do bananas, lemons, mangoes and pineapple from the fruit family. You deserve a treat so drink sugar-free lemonade to chase the blues or munch on diet-friendly yellow jellybeans for a sunny pickup.

CHAKRA: The Yellow Chakra (Solar Plexus) is associated with the pancreas that controls the digestive system, stomach, spleen, gall bladder and lower back. Like the sun the yellow ray descends into the nervous system, the center of feelings and unresolved issues that create stress.

When we attune ourselves to the positive aspects of the yellow ray we begin to alleviate unhealthy symptoms and instead manifest a high level of balance and well being. If the solar plexus center is misused greed and carnal temptations can surface. On the negative side it can mean adverse conditions, such stomach problems or constipation. If the solar plexus are clogged you may need the positive stimulation of yellow to restore balance.

All the good symbolism associated with the Yellow Chakra--the sun, warmth, happiness, life itself--relates to a vibrant constitution and a glowing, friendly personality. Integrity and acts of charity come to the surface as your daily mantra. Your vitality soars and you are full of radiant light and energy.

MUSIC: Color has its own intelligence and musicians tend to describe musical experiences in terms of color. The sound of various instruments resonate with yellow, from light to bright with different tonal sensations. Although Pastel's color organ could flash colored lights in time to music it is not unusual for some individuals to have similar sensations. When sound invokes a sensation of color it is called, "synesthesia," and fortunate are those rare individuals you have that dual listening pleasure. According to C scale standard, the sensation of yellow resonates to the music note "E," and when played on the piano the singer sings 'mi' on the musical scale. Mercury is the planet of this color.

The Russian painter, Wassail Kandinsky said, "The richest lessons are to be learned from music. Hence the current search for rhythm in painting, the way colors are set in motion." In 1912 he produced a 'synthetic' stage show, entitled The Yellow Sound, that combined music by Russian composer Thomas de Hartmann and an extremely complex lighting score.

The next time you listen to music try to visualize the colors that pop up spontaneously in your mind. As you listen to the musical score the yellow ray would certainly be one of the most uplifting sensations of joyful contemplation and enjoyment.

TRIVIA: Friendship blossoms in yellow and signifies a good time friend with an outgoing personality. No wonder yellow roses represent joy and friendship. With yellow on our mind we think of sunny, cheerful vacations and a chance to be carefree and whimsical.

Happy, happy thoughts fill your mind remembering past pleasures. Listening to songs you love can send tension packing. The Beatles' music for "Yellow Submarine" and "Here Comes the Sun" entertain, banish stress and keep us in a jolly mood. Acid Yellow, however, takes us back to 1960s psychedelic art and the youth movement.

Famous yellow-infused paintings recall the Dutch-born, post-impressionist painter, Vincent Van Gogh's *'Yellow Room,'* the famous painting, which depicts his bedroom in Provence, where he lived in a yellow house. Van Gogh (1853-90) used an intense palette of vibrant colors, notably yellow and believed strongly in the emotional immediacy of color sensations.

Does anyone have a sunny voice? Well, celebrated Metropolitan Opera tenor, Marcelo Jordanian, believes there was one singer of remarkable clarity. Commenting in an article in The New York Times about the legendary tenor, Luciano Pavarotti, Jordanian said:

"I remember listening to recordings and hearing the "sun" in his voice."

An exquisite yellow diamond is highly coveted for its rarity, as is yellow sapphire, yellow topaz and yellow amber. Born in November, your birthstone is Vitrine, a sun-kissed stone that boosts a lighthearted attitude that allows you to see the bright side of any situation. Its shimmering glow brings a hint of sunshine to those dull November days. Vitrine was named after the French world for lemon, "citron," to describe its typical yellow color. In terms of adornment, a Vitrine gemstone offers lovers their heart's desire.

Folklore tells us that Vitrine is said to make men handsome and intelligent and sterile women fertile and happy. However, it is best not to rely too much on its magical powers and just settle for Vitrine's jolly disposition.

Blondes are touted to have more fun, though that's debatable. Yet women yearn to be Sun Goddesses and dye their hair blonde or add lightening streaks to their hair to capture the rays of the sun. Let's not forget the legendary screen actress Jean Harlow and Marilyn Monroe or the late Princess Diana-- she conjured up the quintessential image of the Sun Goddess.

We imbibe yellow-infused cocktails and indulge our sweet tooth with lemon ices. Yes, cheerful, inviting, and sometimes sexy, yellow is the essential romantic ingredient to dine by candlelight. When Marlene Dietrich sang Fredric Hollander's "Falling In Love Again," (1930) it was as if the yellow flame ignited her emotions. In her sultry style she lamented:
"Men cluster to me like moths around a flame, and if their wings burn, I know I'm not to blame."
The yellow flame in this refrain is pulsating with erotic emotion.

There's no doubt that yellow with all its happy vibrations is a refreshing new experience. It lifts us mentally into loftier places for creative imagination and scholarly pursuits bringing wisdom and clarity through its vibration.

However, yellow can elicit a sour note and makes us think of a person who is yellow-bellied or a coward. Yellow may even indicate jaundice, sickness or decline in one's health.

Then there's Yellow Journalism, so called when newspapers feature sensational or scandalous items or when ordinary news is sensationally distorted.

The Yellow Peril relates to a danger Western civilization held from expansion of the power and influence of Oriental peoples. Ships raised the Yellow Jack, to indicate a ship in quarantine, and Yellow Fever, connotes a deadly virus transmitted by a mosquito. And a yellow-dog signifies, a mean contemptible personality.

English painter (1775-1851) Joseph Mallory William Turner's rugged landscapes and seascapes were not so much about the objects that he saw, but his abstract treatment of light and the brilliant luminosity that played around his subjects. Commenting on Turner's sun drenched art his detractors accused him of having "yellow fever."

The language of flowers tells us that contrary to modern beliefs the Victorians considered yellow flowers a symbol of jealousy.

This hue has also been linked to Yellow Rage brought on by envy. And let's not forget that during World War II Jewish people were forced to wear the infamous Yellow Star. Keep in mind, therefore, that yellow's duplicity, its positive or negative interpretation, depends upon the context in which the color is presented.

Most significantly Yellow is the most luminous and reflective of the primary colors, the one we count on for revitalization and healing. The life force of the yellow ray of sunshine generates an euphoric feeling of happiness and it restores balance to mind, body and spirit.

As we work in computer driven offices and windowless artificial environments, it becomes even more important to take in the pure energy of sunlight everyday to recharge our body. A break from work at lunchtime or basking in the sun over the weekend will provide all the benefits of the sun's ray, which is the sum total of energy, balance and vitamin D.

Animals seem to instinctively know about the benefits of a sun bath. I have a smart little black dog of the poodle variety (I rescued him from the pound) who finds the perfect spot on a chair or the floor where the sun's rays come through a window, and there he naps in the sun rays each day. Cat's also have that sunny intuition and curl up in the best spot, the sunniest place on the windowsill. Perhaps we need to take a lesson from animal intuition and find a sunny spot to call our own.

Why then hesitate, sunshine happiness can be found in many corners of your imagination. Just take the Yellow Brick Road to the magic kingdom in the Wizard of Oz where adventure awaits your pleasure. The 1939 movie was based on a book by United States novelist and playwright Frank Baum (1856-1919), famous as the author of "The Wonderful Wizard of Oz." He wrote Oz to amuse his children, while staying at the Coronado Hotel near San Diego, CA in 1900.

A melange of yellow flowers can make us feel happier and more connected with the beauty of nature's garden. To feel more optimistic center your gaze on yellow daffodils, tulips, mums or daisies. Breath deeply of their essence it will release feel-good endorphins. Perhaps even remind you of the renewal of spring's yellow bounty, which lets nature's gift of sunshine permeate our lives with unbridled hope and enthusiasm.

THE DYNAMICS OF COLOR
Color Psychology

GOLD
Majestic Ruler

More precious than any other metal
In 'Gold We Trust' do we settle

Conquest of Kings and plunder
Nations glorified no wonder

The Egyptians knew its worth
Cast Gold ingots, gave birth

To majestic wealth for King Tut
Gold-sheathed masks in the cut

Sacred manuscripts inscribed
Glittering gold by a scribe

More Bling than Bling adorned
Gold's intrinsic value scorned

Lavish, luxury and high prestige
Its warm, rich glow we besiege

Enriches noble, grandeur life
Elevates the senses we strife

Golden locks take center stage
Golden girls are all the rage

Precious metal from the earth
Instant wealth we do search

High-end shine, an ingot glow
A powerful symbol this we know

Opulent living, grandiose stuff
This measure of wealth is enough.

Chapter 9
THE DYNAMICS OF COLOR
Color Psychology

GOLD
Majestic Ruler

Gold is noble, it has intrinsic value, it elevates the muses to loftier spheres of golden inspiration. Gold is associated with the Golden Hours of pleasure, of grandeur, extravagance and opulent living to its fullest measure of wealth and luxury. Though gold is not considered a spectrum color it is a darkened brilliant yellow, which by association represents great value and prosperity. It instantly suggests deluxe accouterments and offers high levels of prestige in fashion, product packaging and jewelry.

HISTORY: Gold has a long and exotic history. In ancient cultures gold conveyed status and wealth, warded off evil spirits and even accompanied their owners to the next world. The Egyptians made gold funeral masks for such kings as Tutankhamen of Egypt (1370-1352 B.C.) The Greeks crowned their prized athletes and royal personages with wreaths of pure gold vines and ever since kings and queens and members of their court wore elaborate, gold crowns.

The Spanish conquistadors plundered the gold of the Incas and Mayans for they knew its worth and scribes in the Middle Ages illuminated their sacred manuscripts with fragile and expensive gold leaf. One's value was measured by their weight in gold and kings would tip the scales to demonstrate their enormous worth. Churches brought the religious to their knees, as they perceived gold as the manifestation of God in stained glass liturgical windows depicting biblical allegories.

Gold speaks volumes about how society revered this precious metal that was born in the deep-rooted depths of ancient civilization. Over the ages it has come to represent the quintessential acquisition of wealth. Gold jewelry has its place in history as an exalted and privileged acquisition. In Egypt, Greece and Rome it was the principal adornment worn by royal men and regal women because gold conveyed the standards of status and wealth.

It is interesting to note that many of the same hand tools and techniques forged by craftsmen in ancient cultures, to create jewelry masterpieces, are still used by modern goldsmiths. The gold standard in jewelry in the United States is identified by karats, 22karat being the highest, which means that that there is 22% pure gold in the piece and 2% of another metal alloy. Why? Because 24Karat gold is malleable and it requires the addition of another alloy for strength and durability. The same standard is true for 15 Karat and 10 Karat gold jewelry. Similarly, they are also a compound with another alloy.

Gold plate, however, is not as valuable. It represents a certain thickness of gold electroplated over another metal. Such a piece of jewelry should be identified as 22GP, 15GP or 10GP.

Gold jewelry adds shimmering highlights to most women's complexions. It is a valued accessory worn by stylish women because it is a versatile accessory. It works equally well for evening wear or day wear and also with the casual vibe of jeans and a polo shirt.

Women flaunt their wealth by wearing gold chains, eye-popping gold brooches, bold earrings, bangle bracelets, belts, and rings, singularly as a fashion statement and sometimes they mount several pieces for dramatic impact. The women of India know a thing or two about gold and lavishly decorate their faces, and adorn their hands and body with gold trinkets.

Because of its intrinsic value, when you are tired of the fine gold jewelry you own or it is no longer stylish, you can trade it all in for cash. Seller beware: Just be sure that you are trading with a reputable Better Business Bureau member in the jewelry industry.

FASHION: The runway fashion shows encourage us to adapt the Midas touch and dazzle us with models wearing skin-tight gold stretch tights, gold leather trench coats, gilded evening shoes and handbags, while glittering, gold tiaras adorn the heads of real and would be princesses. A woman encased in a form-fitting gold lame gown, a la Marilyn Monroe, has movie star wealth written allover her curvaceous figure.

You may not want to dip into fashion's gold pot with such extravagance but a stylish silk blouse printed with gold highlights or a gold evening bag and shoes meant for dancing can do wonders to brighten the holidays.

In ancient royal courts the ostentatious display of gold was prolific and glistened on the garments of kings and queens as well as on their dignitaries. Pure gold was appliqued or woven into the fabric of sumptuous ballgowns and decorated lanyards on men's uniforms.

Gold was also embedded into intricate designs of lace collars and cuffs that adorned courtly dress. Taking a cue from the opulence of the nobles, high end designers today create jackets in tweeds with threads that simulate gold for an affluent look that takes you from cocktails to dinner. A posh, wealthy customer can make gold her total fashion image and wear a gold silk shantung designer jacket and a silk chiffon pleated gown a la Givenchy and gild the town in style.

PRODUCTS: The quintessential purveyors of high end merchandise, who want to convey a message of luxury, make sure that gold is an important component in their packaging or label design. Gold lettering on black has dramatic DE lure impact as does maroon with gold ribbons. The trade organization, Only Gold USA supports its jeweler members in an advertisement saying:

"Only gold is treasured, only gold is divine, only gold radiates warmth, only gold inspires legends, only gold defies time."

As such Gold can also be the elixir of imagined wealth. The ultimate cocktail drink has gold flecks floating in the liquid to heighten your enjoyment with golden moments of reverie. The perfume industry also knows a thing or two about the gold standard of this precious metal. They put minuscule gold nuggets in perfume bottles to suggest an aroma with the golden promise of added wealth. Then, too, bakers curl real gold on birthday and wedding cakes to enrich our pleasure.

Cosmetics companies want us all to become "Golden Girls" and add 24-karat flecks of gold in moisturizers to illuminate the complexion. Psychologically it is meant to make us feel enriched by the product and at the same time give us a golden glow.

Gold with its warm, pleasing shimmer makes eyes twinkle and is most flattering to almost all complexions. That is why face powder, eye brow pencils, eye shadows and even lipstick came on the market with glittering gold highlights. Then there's golden blonde hair dye to help us to become golden goddesses simply by adapting the Midas touch in our Goldilocks.

FURNISHINGS: This precious metal in gold leaf applique work decorating the lobby of posh apartment buildings gives the impression that only the upper crust society resides there. In banks gold leaf on the articulation of architectural design conveys the power of money with all the pomp and circumstances of gilded age wealth.

When the historic The Palmer Hilton Hotel in Chicago, Illinois, began an elaborate restoration the Midas touch permeated the luxurious interiors and payed homage to the hotel's French architectural design. The ornate friezes in the famed Empire Room were re-gilded in 24-karat gold, and the room looks much as it did when it opened in 1933. Now with the renovation completed a new generation may bask in the splendor of by-gone elegance. As one patron remembers, "You are never going to see hotels like this again."

Ornate gold leaf frames provide golden highlights and add to the value of a celebrated painter oeuvre, while gold leaf bindings on rare books add value to the classics and first editions. In the law profession gold connotes solid integrity, a value we'd all like to have represent us if we had to go to trial.

Genuine gold threads woven into damask fabric drapes brings rich illumination to a window and when used for upholstery it reflects the salon of a person of considerable fortune. Photo frames fashioned with real gold filigree are an expensive commodity. Don't mistake, however, gold-plated frames for the real thing, they don't have turnover value.

A living room may acquire the Midas touch by merely accessorizing the furnishings with statuesque gold candlesticks or gold tone lampshades to illuminate the room in a gilt theme. Other decorator additions like a gold-plate chandelier, gold-plate light switch and a gold-plated gold brick doorstop enrich the ambiance of any sun goddess' digs.

Then living up to a higher standard, gold tone faucets and metal decor make any bathroom a posh experience.

Eat Your Gold: I just loved the chocolate cake with thin swirls of gold that was presented to me on one of my birthdays. It looked too good to eat but yes, we did, because you can eat gold without any digestive consequences. In Europe, gold is an ingredient in certain arthritis medicine but a prescription may be required. Gold dental work is a rich investment, and a gold crown is the height of affluence.

TRIVIA: Then we all know the Gold Digger, a woman who uses feminine charm to extract money or gifts from men. She is the type that exerts a big pay off in divorce proceedings. Indeed Silence is Golden, because your concentration should not be disturbed when we study in the library, and talking is a 'no no' during the movies.

And then there is the Golden Rule that states that "one should do to others as he would have others do to him." With the advent of Email, the long, leisurely correspondence of history's great lovers like the letters of Elizabeth and Robert Browning or Emily Dickinson's letters to friends, now seems part of another world, a fading reminder of the Golden Age of letter writing.

Let's not forget the legend of the Gold Rush, the 1849 surge of adventurers who went out West in a race for the glitter ore to make their fortune. Sadly many did not, but Levy Strauss did because he set up a tent business, which prospered and eventually he produced denim work clothes that evolved into the famed denim jeans popular today.

Gold coins and gold bar investments are considerably more valuable than printed stock papers as is the Gold Standard, a monetary system with gold of specified weight and fineness as the unit of value. We ascribe the title Gold Bricking to a worker, a shirker who avoids assigned duties or work. And we don't want a Gold Brick, a bar of cheap metal that is not genuine gold.

So revered is gold that we award the highest recognition, the Gold Medal to a person or team members who come out first in a competition or tournament. We also hear of the Gold Standard medical exam that is considered the best and most thorough and complete evaluation of our health.

When your employer wants you to take retirement the Golden Handshake is the severance pay offered to an older employee and the Gold Watch retirement token recognizes faithful service rendered. Yet key executives get a Golden Parachute that guarantees them substantial financial benefits. Then we'd all like to have a Golden Rent, at a fixed rate that cannot be changed.

A celebrated singer may be described as having a Golden Voice. Beverly Sills (1929-2007) the American diva comes to mind. She sang a prolific repertoire and her golden voice was heard in diverse roles at the Metropolitan Opera and all over the world. Later she became the managing director of the New York City Opera.

Living on the Gold Coast says you've reached the pinnacle of success and can afford to live in a wealthy residential area, and the Golden Age denotes a specifically wonderful era in your life. In retirement years many seniors experience their Golden Years of carefree happiness.

A plain gold wedding ring, usually inscribed with some sentimental message inside, symbolizes the intrinsic value of the marriage and when the couple reaches their 50th year together they celebrate their Golden Wedding anniversary. Then there is the Golden Retriever that lovable and loyal dog so popular today.

In fine art, the Golden Section, is the perfect position that avoids extremes, the happy medium. In the landscape "Sunset in the Mountains" (1859), the German born American painter, Albert Interstate (1830-1902) infuses a gem-like golden sunset. Created to astound the viewer, the artist's depiction of light moves one's gaze from the glistening rocks in the foreground, along the serpentine river, and to the hazy golden sky beyond.

On the contrary, the Golden Gate Bridge in San Francisco is not even painted gold, but the reflection of the sun makes it glow like gold.

Let's not forget the famed "Oscar," the golden statuette awarded annually by the Academy of Motion Picture Arts and Sciences for achievement in motion pictures. Or "Glitter and Be Gay" the lively aria from the operetta, "Candide" (l956), which says it all in a hilarious and provocative jewelry aria.

Based on Voltaire's brilliant satire of human folly, written in 1759, the operetta's music by famed American composer/conductor, Leonard Bernstein (1918-90) was his greatest creation. Classical Music wrote, "It reflected the 1950s trend for cross-fertilization between the Broadway musical on one hand and "straight" theater and opera on the other."

Alas Gold by any other name would not be as magical, as valuable,or as highly coveted. It's like a magic carpet fairy tale that takes us on a journey to the Golden Kingdom of an imaginary world. As a highly exalted metal, to the enlightened gold elevates believers to the sphere of Godliness, while here on earth it gives a Golden Opportunity to those lucky mortals who lead a twenty-four-karat lifestyle of wealth, luxury and prestige.

"In the harmony of sound, the harmony of color,

even the harmony motion itself, its beauty is all akin to

that expression of the soul-self in the harmony of the

mind , if used properly in relationship to the body."

-Edgar Cayce

THE DYNAMICS OF COLOR
Color Psychology

ORANGE
Joyful Wisdom

Orange may lack the passion of red
A luminous interest in life instead

A cheery spirit and winsome style
Sociable and gregarious for awhile

Pumpkin to peach produces smiles
Well being, vitality for miles

Think melon, mango and apricot
Carrots, drink vitamin C a lot

Yellow wisdom within its core
A joyful orange never a bore

The color of creative expression
Stimulates ideas, did I mention

It signifies glory and self-esteem
New feelings of optimism we glean

Wear orange and attract attention
Warm up friendships and connection

Kind and friendly, ready to assist
Orange folks overdo, must resist

Giving in to everyone's demand
Protect yourself, they'll understand

Your easygoing nature is to blame
Orange generosity ignites the flame

Bright is your future in orange glow
Happier, self-confident this we know.

THE DYNAMICS OF COLOR
Color Psychology

ORANGE
Joyful Wisdom

Mother Nature displays her best orange flavors in fall colors that burst on the scene as the season changes to autumn in blazing sugar maples, copper moons and honeyed sunsets. Fields of pumpkins everywhere signal the holidays, Halloween and Thanksgiving, and autumn engages our senses with the aroma of exotic spices, gingerbread cookies and hot apple cider welcoming us to the warm, blazing fireplace.

The spectacle of autumn has inspired countless poets, musicians and artists. In his 1831 poem, "Autumn Woods," American poet and journalist, William Cullen Bryant (1794-1878) emphasized the importance of autumn in America, and celebrates fall in this poem:

> *"The woods of Autumn, all around our vale,*
> *Have put their glory on.*
> *The mountains that unfold,*
> *In their wide sweep, the colored landscape round,*
> *Some groups of giant kings, purple and gold,*
> *That guard the enchanted ground."*

Robust Color: In celebration of orange we may also consider the robust colors of the Tuscan countryside, the blood orange sunset of the American Southwest, the image of the sweet oranges of Florida and the tangy oranges of Seville. Wherever you look, orange influences a myriad of products. There are tints, tones and shades of orange from hot orange to burnt sugar to cinnamon and rustic terracotta variations in apparel to home furnishings and even automobiles.

Though bright orange is often a misunderstood color, think of the delicious fruity possibilities: mango, papaya, nectarine, persimmon, melon, sweet cantaloupe and the more livable colors such as carrot, butternut squash, pumpkin, delicate peach, tangerine, apricot, coral or orange sherbet.

PERSONALITY: Orange is a joyful color and with it you feel happy with unbridled energy and enthusiasm. You're a born "nob Vivian," you have a winsome manner and, like citrus orange, you have zest for life. You're a fun loving extrovert and like to be around people and they, in a similar manner, love to be around you.

Orange symbolically represents an adventurous spirit, a risk taker, a person who isn't afraid to make fast decisions and take a new idea to new levels of excitement. Such an individual has the "smarts" and is usually the brainy one in the crowd who exudes confidence and professionalism.

The orange ray fosters enlightenment and helps the creative individual to become a mental giant, a free thinker, dynamic and alert, bursting with energy. Fiery orange dispels limitation and aids in the assimilation of new ideas.

In the workplace orange suggests a quick smile and a good-matured approach to team projects. You're a good organizer and competence in dealing with co-workers. However, wishing to be agreeable you may be inclined to be a giver rather than a taker. Obsequious, perhaps to a fault, the orange individual often defers to others' wishes or opinions, and in so doing they are sometimes neglectful of their own wants and desires.

Nothing is ordinary about the orange personality. They attract scores of acquaintances and therefore may sometimes appear to be fickle, but that is not true. However, they do cherish and treasure loyal friends. The orange individual prefers unusual places and special surroundings. They like to work things out to perfection so that friends will admire their exquisite taste in food and furnishings.

ORIGINS: Every color story has its origins from the rainbow to myths and legends. Orange is a secondary color, created by combining the two primary colors yellow and red, and as such this smart and sassy color shares the beneficial rays of yellow (the intellect) and red (the energizer). The color temperature of orange is warm. It may not give you the passion of red, but it does give you wisdom of yellow.

Juicy, fruity Orange is a Middle English word, from the old French orange, from the Arabic Parana, from Persian Angara and from Sanskrit Angara, orange tree having fragrant white flowers and the round fruit with a yellowish-red rind and a sectioned, pulpy interior.

Orange is strongly orientated toward food. It conjures up the image of fast food restaurants decorated in orange and red. Why? Because orange stimulates appetite while red energizes people to eat in a hurry and these two colors combined promote quick table turnover. In casinos and nightclubs the use of bright orange in design articulation has another meaning. Similarly it has a purpose, to encourage gamblers to linger longer and stay in the game.

HISTORY: Until the seventeenth century, the word *orange* was associated only with the citrus fruit, which had first been imported from India in the tenth century.

According to Hope and Walsh in the Color Compendium, at some point during the seventeenth century, orange gained a sexual connotation. For instance, Nell Gwyn (1650-87) is thought to have seduced Britain's Charles II (1630-85) with the oranges (still rare at that time) that she was selling. Since then both the fruit and the color were used often in erotic paintings.

Historically oranges and orange blossoms have been symbols of love and potions to elicit love. The French custom of throwing orange blossoms over brides symbolized fertility, as few trees are more fruitful than the orange. French brides adopted the custom and wore orange blossoms in their hair or carried them in bouquets. The courtesans knew a thing or two about this rare elixir of love and sprinkled their sheets with orange perfume and bathed in orange scented waters.

Redheads had their day in ancient Rome, where red (or orange) hair was popular. Bleach and henna were used to modify dark hair colors. Lucille Ball may have appeared zany and funny but her timing was sheer genius. Hillary Clinton, on the other hand, has the genius of Orange with a grounding and maturity that made her an ideal contender for the role of First Lad y. However, such a destination was not fulfilled.

A Family called Orange: There once was a princely European family, called Orange, the rulers of the Netherlands and a leader in European culture, commerce and colonialism. In 1677 William III, (1650-1702) known as "William of Orange," a stallholder of the United Provinces of the Netherlands married Mary, daughter of James II (1685-88), King of England, Scotland and Ireland.

Then, too, in 1688 William III was asked by the opposition to James to invade England. Thus victorious he became king of England, ruling in the United Kingdom from 1688-94. He was proclaimed joint monarch with his wife Mary II after James fled.

Then there are the Orange men, Irish Protestants, especially of Northern Ireland, so called after William, Prince of Orange.

Orange is a favorite. It is also the name of a town in Clause department, in southeastern France. Founded by Charlemagne, it was the seat of the House of Orange. Orange claims the name for several cities in the United States: in South West California, near Los Angeles; in New Jersey near Newark; a city in South East Texas and a town in South Connecticut to name a few.

Academia also has its color codes. Of the palette of eight colors to identify the major faculties of American Universities Orange is designated for engineering.

CHAKRA: The Orange Chakra (The Spleen), located between the navel and the genitals, controls the splenetic center in the body and the digestive system. This Chakra also called, sacra, rules the lower intestines, kidneys, reproductive organs and potency.

Orange hue vibrations bath this Chakra and the body with positive action, directing the yellow charged wavelength towards mental rejuvenation and the energy charged red vibration towards good health.

As a tonic for mental debility, orange can awaken new hope, new courage and foster greater stability. On the negative side, suspicion is an emotion that is held in the abdominal region. However, by bringing in contemplation on the orange ray this emotion can be softened and released.

The sensation of abundance that floods the digestive system through the orange ray increases appetite and may cause overindulgence and weight problems. The orange stimulant explains why fast food restaurants and cafeterias choose orange for decor and packaging. Over stimulation of orange may also be identified with a person who is a food binge or has a bulimic condition.

To maintain normal weight or if you are dieting avoid orange decor and eat on blue plates and surround yourself with the calm, cool indulgence of other less stimulating colors.

MUSIC: Color can cut through the mundane with its own special magic. It can have the effect of amazing sound, amplifying a crystalline bell tone and crash its way into your senses or it can soothe and lull you to peaceful reverie.

The Color Compendium describes how certain artists have tried to articulate their own impression about movement and music.

The Russian abstract painter Wassail Kandinsky (1866-1944) attributed warm orange as possessing greater movement than the cool blues and greens. In trying to describe the physical effects of color he linked colors with the sounds of musical instruments, designating orange as a church bell or strong contralto voice.

There have been many efforts to correlate musical notes with the colors of the spectrum. Sir Issac Newton, who beamed seven colors of the rainbow through a prism chose seven notes of the musical scale: note "D" was orange on the C scale and in Correggio is sung as "Re."

Orange with its components of fiery red and stimulating yellow is an exuberant color and as such might well be likened to the opera, "Carmen" by French composer George Bizet (1838-75), which premiered in Paris in 1875. Considered, the first realistic opera, the plot was inspired by Prosper Merriment's short novel about a passionate Spanish gypsy. It shocked the first audiences with it lifelike characters, sensual passions and graphic on-stage murder. Although the opera remains popular on the opera repertoire the book, "Classical Music" wrote:

"Shocked by its raw realism, the first critics reacted coolly, disappointing Bizet, who died before it became a box-office hit."

Music can also be the softest sound around and invoke images of melancholia and allude to the precious, short days of the season. Such an image reminds me of "Autumn Leaves," the French song, "Les Guileless Tortes" (literally "Dead Leaves") with lyrics by French poet Jacques Revert and music by Joseph Zosma. The English lyrics by Johnny Mercer (1947) made Autumn Leaves a popular ballad:

"The Falling leaves drift by my window, the autumn leaves of red and gold, I see your lips, the summer kisses, the sun-burned hands I used to hold. Since you went away the days grow long, and soon I'll hear old winter's song, but I miss you most of all my darling, when autumn leaves start to fall."

Many other songs invoke similar sentiments such as "Autumn in New York, (1934)by Vernon Duke, which engages us to remember the splendor of autumn leaves.

MEDITATION: Thinking of your body as musical instrument that you can tune up with the orange ray in meditation. First you will need to find a quiet and private space in which to perform this exercise. Do a few stretches before you begin to open up your body to receive the orange ray and musical note sensation. You'll also need a small pitch pipe (available from a music store) or if you have a piano you can play the note "D" on the C Scale. On either instrument play the "D" note and concentrate on the sound and its relationship to the orange ray.

As you play the "D" musical keynote. in tune with your image of orange ray, try to visualize your heart's desire. Be it reasons for health, ambition or energized lifestyle you have a wide range of aspirations that may be opened up through the orange/D note connection.

After performing this ensemble meditation don't expect immediate results. Remember the old adage, "How do I get to Carnegie Hall?" The answer: "Practice, practice, practice." The same is true for this exercise.

Orchestrating the benefits of music and color, in this case orange, will open up your joyful nature, stimulate enthusiasm, steady your nerves and instill confidence. Of course, as with all disciplines, this meditation depends on your belief in the practice of color and music therapy.

FASHION: Bright orange is a powerful color and as such women sometimes shy away from it, thinking they can not wear it because it is not flattering. This is not true. Bright orange is a stand out color, it says you're an extrovert, a go-fetter who has fashion savvy and wears it with confidence.

Orange also works well in combination with colors plucked from autumn leaves. Think of adding forest green, goldenrod, crimson, deep burgundy or brown to the mix. A sporty jacket in terracotta with forest green pants and a rust colored turtleneck looks rustic and outdoorsy. It says you are the kind of person who is approachable and friendly.

Autumn color also works well for men engaged in the creative fields of the corporate world. They can adopt the same colors and wardrobe pieces for weekend wear or casual Fridays.

To tame the flame of bright orange other options are available from flattering tints to soft earth shades. However, you don't have to look like Halloween or a Thanksgiving pumpkin, but just like an artist's palette, you can reflect nature in all its autumn glory.

Artists of the Hudson River School were colorful interpreters of American's autumn countryside. In the painting, "Autumn" 1853, the artist, Frederic Edwin Church (1826-1900), in his desire to portray a true American landscape, created a masterpiece, a brilliant evocation of fall, a season whose colors are a sublime vision of serene nature. Harmonized tones of copper, forest green, burnt sienna, and brilliant crimson evoke breathtaking scenery in the full triumph of autumn in its most resplendent hues.

FASHION: Similarly fashion also takes its inspiration from nature and offers a wide range of orange possibilities. Visualize the autumn leaves that inspire flattering shades of burnt peachy rust and brown infused orange and golden sunlight in fashion ensembles.

A tailored wool dress in a deep rusty-orange shade is conservative and autumnal. It says you are serious and businesslike, a person who is warm-heated and a good team player. You have a gregarious personality, who keeps everyone snapping to attention, in an atmosphere of cooperation that makes work far more pleasant each day. Why? Because deep rust has the energy of red and the brightness of orange with the grounding of brown in its formula, and like autumn leaves you project a powerful multi-faceted persona.

Pumpkin color looks chic and sophisticated in a blazer coordinated with steel gray wool pants and a shimmering gray silk blouse. The look has executive punch and is elegant for town wear. Add a gray suede tote and you're ready from day into night with a powerful sense of confidence and well being.

Men also look great in autumnal colors. A dark pumpkin, suede bomber jacket with gray trousers and a gray turtleneck, says he's coordinated with executive punch for casual Fridays.

By evening the desire for more sumptuous outfits calls for a dramatic approach to enriching your image. The total effect of the color amber with highlights of gold has stunning impact, especially on auburn haired women. Wear a shimmering amber rust taffeta strapless evening gown with a matching stole and sweep onto the dance floor as your magnetic amber ensemble garners all eyes' approval. Add a necklace of Russian amber jewelry and the look is elegant and breathtaking.

Be adventurous and don't be intimidated by orange. Tints of peach, coral and cantaloupe are dainty, feminine versions of orange that create a sunny disposition for any woman. A creamy peach silk blouse softens a black suit and transforms it into an ensemble for a night on the town.

Wear coral with brown and its warm glow says you're down to earth and reliable. Get on the wild side of fashion and coordinate with handbag and shoes in leopard spots or orange-themed tiger prints.

HOME FURNISHINGS: Tasteful shades of orange have livable qualities that make the home environment seemingly dwell in the autumn sanctuary of the great outdoors. A living room, painted in a deep, harvest tone, like paprika, may not be for everyone, but its rich impression provides a warm and hospitable ambiance, grounded in solid hospitality. When coordinated with the warm brown classic wood furniture, scenic autumnal paintings and treasured antiques, the warmed up environment is cozy and says you're a thoughtful hostess who loves to have company.

Spicy terracotta has bedroom appeal and can have Southwestern charm or the ethnicity of Mexico, Morocco or India. Such a room provides an opportunity to show off your ethnic pride by decorating the space with personal collectibles, earthenware pottery or old world antiques. Do something unexpected. Paint a wood bed frame in terracotta, then dress the bed with turquoise blue bed linens and pillows. The look balances the warmth of terracotta with the cool, calm serenity of blue. Walls painted in soft misty peach create a cocoon, a safe haven and a personal expression of your ethnic heritage.

In a child's room you can sweeten your time together with a juicy fruit splash of orange. All you need do is to paint a rocking chair or toy box orange and it will brighten any playtime together with the perfect balance of harmony and happy activity. A comfy sitting area can acquire an autumnal feeling with amber wicker furniture and cozy rusty-brown corduroy seat cushions.

Kitchens are another case altogether. It is not only a place where you can display your personal taste and culinary sense, it's a reflection on the way you live. Pure orange is an appetite accelerator and as such it is not a good wall paint choice. However, walls can be more effective and appealing in soft coral or pale peach, which are the colors used by posh, high-end restaurants.

You can easily emulate high-end restaurant decor by painting kitchen cabinets coral or peach. The addition of pumpkin trim to articulate design elements provides a complementary contrast. To elevate the ceiling choose a creamy peach tint for height and spaciousness. The look conveys a sheltering and warm ambiance that says, "welcome."

If you are timid about going with orange or any of its tints, tones or shades you can shop for counter top, kitchen equipment in vivid bright orange: blenders, juicers, toasters to name a few. The color orange stimulates activity and boosts energy in food preparation in most kitchens.

Obviously there are many harvest incentives for home decorators to consider. A jolt of juicy vibrant orange can boost energy while softer tints can tame tension and create a sweeter ambiance that is intimate and calming. Your home is an expression of your hospitality and affable hostess skills.

Deciding on the right orange-based color for a dining room is essential to invoke good vibrations that can make the whole family and guests feel more relaxed. Think of the more livable appeal of soft coral, peach, mango or papaya. All it takes evoke a new vibe is to merely paint the dining room walls in any one of these harmony-boosting tints to make dining a peaceful pleasure.

Your color decision depends on the kind of dining table, chairs and hutch that you already have and also the kind of lighting system you have installed in the room. Sunlight streaming in by day in a peachy dining room can be charming, but will look quite different at night under incandescent lighting which throws a yellow-based glow over the room.

A fluorescent lighting system will cast a blue tinged glow over the room and that will make a peachy color look cool, and to some people it will create an unappealing and unappetizing atmosphere. The best advice is to take color chip samples of the orange-based tints and tack them up on the dining room wall before you paint. Wait a few days and observe how the orange-based color appeals to you by day and also observe it by night when the room is lit by you home or apartment's specific lighting system.

PRODUCTS: Marketing specialists know that a yellow-based orange product is not an incentive boosting color. WHY? Because it is seen as inexpensive and is often used in cheap motels and fast food chains. However, orange makes it easier to find desk top accessories, like staplers and rulers when they're in bright orange because of their high intensity visibility. Similarly with so many household-cleaning products on the market shelves, "Tide" draws customer attention with the high visibility of bright reddish/orange.

To invoke richness and quality designers chose deep rust shades, terracotta and pumpkin for a wide variety of home products. White dinnerware may be practical, but brick colored round and square dinnerware, like the "Fiesta" brand turn an ordinary dinner into a festive fall occasion. Architectural Moorish tile designs, in orange and white porcelain give new meaning to a dining without adding extra calories.

Eco-friendly towels let you wrap yourself up in orange bath towels made of rayon from bamboo and combed Egyptian cotton. Why bamboo? It absorbs faster than cotton.

Underfoot in any room, a rug can seemingly turns up the heat, especially when it is an art-inspired creation and a lush high-pile chrysanthemum pops open on a sunny terracotta low-pile field. Autumnal accents like spice aroma candles, or a bunch of fall leaves in a hallowed-out butternut squash vase makes the splendor of orange infusion last a bit longer.

The corporate world has orange ambition and is the color of choice for "Yes to Carrots," a parable-free personal care natural product line. What's more the fun-loving young entrepreneur has cultivated a wardrobe of bright orange pieces. Even the firms San Francisco-based, global headquarters incorporates the brand's signature color in 'Yes to Carrots' staplers and pencils. His business card reads, "chief carrot lover."

EAT YOUR COLORS: The autumn bounty of orange veggies and fruits just keeps getting better and better each season and the best picks are at green farmers markets. Pumpkins, it turns out, are packed with fiber, folic acid, calcium and contain carotene and vitamin C, potent antioxidants that protect and repair cells. Other autumn vegetables like carrots and sweet potatoes also contain antioxidants, which keep the brain cells strong and healthy. Of course, colorful healthy meals should include other 'in season' veggies like broccoli, Brussels sprouts and collard greens.

Orange options also permeate the beauty trade. Classic coral is elegant and can warm up the pale to medium skin tone with soft blush, creamy eye shadow and/a very Grace Kelly signature lipstick. Bolder shades like terracotta, warmed rust or bronzier tones complement darker skin tones and can be found on most cosmetic counters in major department stores. However, for the economy minded drug store brands offer a varied palette to suit every complexion. The fall harvest is also rich in magnesium found in winter squash, rutabagas and beets.

However, to get your essential vitamins, minerals and nutrients, don't think that fall is the only season of plenty. Farmer's are filling the green markets year-round with nutritious produce. Manhattan, New York, nutritionist Reyna Franco says, "Foods that are 'not shipped' thousands of miles are fresher than and have a higher nutrient value."

TRIVIA: Nature's color show is free for the viewing. Fall foliage, that explosion of color come autumn makes many of us head for the great outdoors to witness the phenomenon of the autumn leaves that change to a panorama of brilliant hues. Once green the gold to fiery red leaves appear in sugar maples, red oaks, firs and other indigenous trees throughout the United States and people come from all over the world to bask in the glorious display of autumn colors.

So why do autumn leaves change colors? Scientific analysis tells us that the chlorophyll that has been pumping through the green leaves all summer, reacting with light and heat to make food for the plant, begins to break down. And, as the green pigment drains away, the yellow pigments that have been there all along are unmasked. The leaves then turn from green to golden orange and fiery red thanks to hormonal changes that are prompted by progressively shorter days and cooler temperatures.

Then there's Indian Corn with its variegated kernels of autumn colors to decorate and celebrate the fall holidays, and in late October or early November we can enjoy the mild weather on an Indian Summer day. Perhaps we should sing the "Indian Love Call," the ballad of autumn love. That is the time of the moon and the year, when love dreams to Indian maidens appear, and this the song that they hear:

"When I'm Calling You oo-oo-oo, oo-oo-oo, Will you answer too--oo-oo-oo, oo-oo-oo,'"

This haunting melody lived on in the hearts of music lover's is based on Rudolf Friml, book and lyrics by the famed team Otto Harbach and Oscar Hemmmerstein, 2nd.

The Museum of the City of New York, the bastion of the history of the city of New York, chose orange in 2004 as its logo and signature color mainly because it is one of the colors featured in the official New York City flag. (The other two are blue and white).

The national organization, The American Society for the Prevention of Cruelty to Animals identifies with orange in the fight against animal abuse, while "Mission Orange," represents the mission to prevent pet over-population nationwide.

Orange also has some alarming but important vibes. It has come to suggest danger and a call for attention. In America, orange is often used for safety garments because of its high visibility, said to be even greater than yellow. Hunters in the woods wear eye-popping garments of near-phosphorescent orange as do policemen, construction workers, bicyclists. Similarly life jackets are bright orange because people can be seen in dark waters. Lately I noticed an orange flag on a pole on a mobile wheelchair to signal pedestrians to make way. Orange cones on the street can represent a real hazard and alert us to step aside.

Orange is an attention grabbing color. Picture those Hare Krishna sect members dancing and chanting on a city street wearing light-orange robes that command one's interest.

Orange is the color of hunger awareness and is a campaign color of the Food Bank for New York, which is part of Feeding American, a national major hunger relief organization. The color choice makes sense when you think about orange as an appetite stimulant. When a celebrity chef, like Mario Batali wears orange as a badge of honor in his work space, it gives new status to the meaning of orange in restaurants.

Sports uniforms also favor attention-grabbing orange. From the Olympic athletes to the players on the baseball and football fields orange demands to be noticed. For example, the Baltimore Orioles wear orange and black, the New York Mets, orange and blue.

Orange continues to filter through popular vocabulary. Who can forget the 1971 movie thriller Clockwork Orange based on the 1962 novel, by British author, Anthony Burgess. It shocked people's senses with strange and fantastic imagery. Then adding to the gore, the term Agent Orange, reminds us of the powerful toxic herbicide used in Vietnam.

If orange could ever be more musically celebrated think no further than the "The Love of Three Oranges," written in 1921 by Russian composer, Sergei Prokofiev (1891-1953). The only one of his operas to win international fame it is a delightful tale about the search for three oranges, a wicked witch and a Princess, of course. According to the book *Classical Music*, "Prokofiev had a childlike playfulness, shown in a fondness for primary-color orchestration."

On a more subtle note, to quell our emotions, lets imbibe Orange pekoe tea, and drink plenty of OJ for our daily dose of vitamin C. Then on hot days drink orangeade and in the autumn enjoy a mugful of apple cider with a cinnamon stick. Speaking of stick, we can prune our cuticles with an Orange Stick.

The scent of orange can be had with aromas such as sandalwood, Ylang-Ylang, Damiana and Gardenia. Candles with fruity orange undertones may waft though the house with an inviting autumn aroma.

If you need another dose of orange just look at the multi colored, exotic parrots who wear orange in the proud plumage of their feathers. With plumage of another kind, we can easily recognize the shopping bags and packages from Hermes, the famed purveyor of luxury products, whose signature color is orange.

Did you know that you can eliminate toxic indoor air with simple house plants like chrysanthemums that fend off cigarette smoke and other pollutants. If all else fails to draw you to orange, look at the world through orange colored glasses to see joy and happiness unfolding. If you live by the ocean search for orange sea glass and gaze at the color to refresh, recharge and pump up your enthusiasm and zest for life.

Chapter 11
THE DYNAMICS OF COLOR
Color Psychology

TANGERINE
Sun-kissed Femininity

Tangerine lives next to red
A sunny hue, softer instead

A citrus splash and fruity
Tangy, tarty, perky juicy

Think of a sun-kissed breeze
Carefree days, easy-to-please

Lovers of tangerine glean
Friendships long and lean

A sunny glimpse of Tangerine
Is fashion forward and serene

Shedding a light orange glow
Softens the complexion we know

Tangerine's a youthful tint
New ideas, here's the hint

Tames orange's exuberance
Adds a sweet countenance

Juicy ideas are overflowing
Romantic Tangerine is showing

A splash of tangerine uplifts
Coaxes affection and a kiss.

Chapter II
THE DYNAMICS OF COLOR
Color Psychology

TANGERINE
Sun-Kissed Femininity

Tangerine, a cousin of Orange, lives next to red and basks in sun-kissed yellow with a reddish hue. Like the delicious fruit, this color represents everything that is sweet, perky and gay. Such a color has youthful abandon written all over its character with a splash of laughter that reminds us of teenagers giggling.

According to the renowned American artist, Laurie Zagon, in "It's Never Too late to Have a Happy Childhood," tangerine helps us to pave the way to renewing child-like discovery. In the book with the same eponymous title, Ms. Zagon's color-saturated abstract paintings are paired with Claudia Black's profound insights. One such painting called "Window to Destiny" (1988) is accompanied with the message:

"You were once a wondrous, joyous, creative, curious, innocent child. That special inner child remains with you today. Honor, celebrate, and acknowledge that child."

It's plain to see that tangerine has a lot going for it and of all the colors under the sun it allows you to come out and play with beams of laughter. A person who loves tangerine has unbridled enthusiasm and wakes up every morning laughing and eager to get on their merry way. Tangerine can make us feel willy-nilly at times, cause this citrus-y color can turn up the excitement and It never fails to perk up even the dullest day.

ORIGIN: The word tangerine has a dualistic origin. The Chinese called it "mandarin," perhaps channeling the proud Chinese public officials, the Mandarins, comparing the color of the yellow robes they wore to the fruit on the tree.

The small citrus tree, Citrus reticulata, native to China, bears lance-shaped leaves and orange-yellow to deep orange-yellow loose-skinned fruit with sweet, juicy pulp. Some varieties are called simply Mandarin or Mandarin Oranges. The French word for mandarin orange is "mandarine."

And herein lies the second version. The French word tanger, refers to Tangier, Morocco which was administered as an international zone from 1923-1924 by the France, Britain and Spain. The French may have christened the name tangerine to represent the exotic, juicy fruit that was cultivated in Tangier in ancient times.

A port city, Tangier is located on the Moroccan side of the Strait of Gibraltar. It was an Old World Phoenician city, which was held from 1471 to 1928 by different European countries. However, the city's international status was restored after World War II and in 1956 it was returned to Morocco.

So whether we call it Mandarine, Mandarin or tangerine, orange by any other name it would not conjure up such tales of its exotic origin.

MUSIC: Juicy, tarty tangerine has had several incarnations in music. Did you know that the tune "Tangerine" was background music in the movie Star Trek III: The search for Spock? The popular song, "Tangerine," was published in 1941 with music by Victor Schertzinger and refreshing lyrics by Johnny Mercer, but the most popular recorded version of the song was made by the Jimmy Dorsey Orchestra in 1942. A disco instrumental version by the Salsoul Orchestra revived the song, bringing it to the top twenty in 1976. Here's the chorus:

"Tangerine, Tangerine, living reflection from a dream, I was her love, she was my queen, and now a thousand years between. Thinking how it used to be, does she still remember times like these? To think of us again? And I do."

The tune goes on with the Herb Albert & The Tijuana Brass, which recorded a leisurely-paced version of the song for their album, "Whipped Cream & Other Delights."

If you want to hear and see how the song Tangerine was introduced on the screen, track down the 1942 Paramount movie, "The Fleets In." It starred a cast of old time headliners, Dorothy Lamour, William Holden, Eddie Bracken, singer Cass Daley, and Betty Hutton in her feature film debut.

FASHION: Tangerine has come full circle in fashion collections and is no longer considered as being a hard-to-wear color. It is especially flattering on women whose complexions range from mellow tan to deep bronze. They can look fabulous wearing flirty cocktail dresses.

The brilliant tangerine hue puts a zing into a sleeveless mandarin collar, knee-length lace dress.

The dress lined discreetly with a skin-toned mini slip reveals a woman's shapely legs. Created by the bad boy of Paris, French fashion designer Jean-Paul Gaultier, American knock-offs of the same dress took gals to cocktail parties in autumn style. The look says you're a fun loving person who likes to dazzle eye-watchers with tangy, tarty, pizzazz.

When it comes to career apparel deep tangerine is a stunning look in a fashionable jacket with flair sleeves. Worn with an earthy brown kick-pleat skirt or cigarette-slim pants the ensemble captures the autumnal look with sophistication. It says you're a warm-hearted career woman who is grounded in professionalism.

As for men, a suede tailored jacket in a very deep tangerine shade gives the masculine edge to office wear with warm, executive vibes.

As the chill of autumn turns to winter a tangerine wool coat with a large funnel collar makes a toasty, stylish statement that says you're on target with style and sensibility.

HOME FURNISHINGS: Tangerine can make a guest room look fresh,youthful and inviting. The question is how to decorate without over juicing the interior. White walls and white sheer curtains on windows tied back with tangerine ribbon and small imitation marigold bouquets begin the tangerine dream and let the sunshine in. A daybed wearing a quilted tangerine coverlet perks up the sleeping area, and when contrasted with pristine white bed linens the look is clean and serene.

Bring in decorator touches such as a vase of marigolds on a side table, and hang colorful white-framed modern abstract artwork on the walls. The tangerine and white treatment reminds us of an old fashioned orange creamsicle. The sweet, simplicity of it all assures a pleasant ambiance.

EAT YOUR COLORS: Refreshing as an orange sherbet and as delicious as mango can be you'll still need more than tangerine colors in your meal mix. So don't forget butternut squash, carrots, zesty orange juice and peaches to fuel your appetite with provide good nutrition.

LITERATURE: Tangerine gets academic kudos as a novel for young readers. When English teacher and author Edward Bloor wrote the book, "Tangerine," he set the story in Tangerine, Florida. The hardcover book was published in 1997 by Harcourt Brace & Company. Focusing on the tangerine growing region of Florida, the novel touches on environmental and social issues critical at the time.

It explored the trials of Paul Fisher, its legally blind soccer-playing protagonist. Environmental issues may still plague the tangerine area. To learn more about the subject check the book out at your local library.

Let's raise the bar for tangerine, that it not stand alone but partner to orange in bringing laughter and song into our universe. After all, tangy, tasty tangerine can be as animated as frothy orangeade, it can soothe and lull us into orange sherbet dreams, and it can be cool as an orange creamsicle.

It is interesting to note that in New York City on West 41st street, The Times Center's entrance walls appear to be a sun kissed tangerine. The Center, however, describes the wall color as a "marigold."

The wall color is driven by an undertone of red that moves people forward while the mellow tint of tangerine conveys the message, 'welcome' and the impression that something special is going on here. Obviously the tangerine infused color does just that, because The Times Center presents exciting live events year round including TimesTalks, concerts and diverse intellectual platforms.

"Red is one of the strongest colors, it's blood, it has a power with the eye, that's why traffic lights are red I guess, and stop signs as well. In fact, I use red in all my paintings."

-Keith Haring

Chapter 12
THE DYNAMICS OF COLOR
Color Psychology

RED
The Power Color

Stop, pay attention Red declares
Its drama, energy causes stares

An attention-grabber sexy, too
Something notable happens to you

Humming with vitality and vigor
Passionate Reds a svelte figure

The color of power top of the list
High-achievers conquer, take risks

An extrovert personality drives
But competition helps you thrive

Action-oriented, bold facilitator
Strong willed can be a dictator

Red signals 'Stop' and danger
Protects, wards off a stranger

Anger reaction, 'I see Red'
Need to cool down go to bed

Forget the morning coffee break
Re-energize on red and meditate

Toast to the glory of red emotions
Rich, radiant an brilliant notions

Passionate, sexy, a show stopper
Pure red makes our lives even hotter.

Chapter 12
THE DYNAMICS OF COLOR
Color Psychology

RED
The Power Color

Red is a bold, powerful, exiting and beautiful color that pulsates with strength, vitality and sexual passion. Its vibration is associated with creation itself and the very lifeblood of our existence. Red is a vibrant primary color and can crash its way into our senses with new images, new emotions and a special magic.

Jules Guerin, noted color expert and muralist, proved beyond a doubt, that red is a color that excites the mind. For instance he said: "It is impossible to sit in a bright red room for any length of time without feeling restless and uncomfortable. Red cuts through the silence and demands attention."

The color temperature is red hot denoting heat, strength, energy and vitality. This hue says STOP, there's something exciting going on here, yet as a warning it signals danger.

Red is located at one end of the visual spectrum and as such it has a wavelength that registers longer in a person's visual perception. People not only see red, but their senses perk up and they feel its intoxicating vibrations through the Red, Root Chakra, in music, in the food they eat and in the products they purchase. Red clothing choices tell another stimulating story, as do the red décor in the home or office environment.

Visualizing red has profound affect on health and a positive outlook. When the brain interprets the red wavelengths, it causes the pituitary gland to send out signals to the adrenal glands, creating a rise in blood pressure, respiration rate and heartbeat. Too much red can be over stimulating and the abundant energy flow may need to be channeled into productive outlets. Such a person might consider becoming an activist, head up volunteerism opportunities or challenge with a new hobby.

INFLUENCE: Red works into our lives in bright red for drama, berry red for clarity, ruby for richness, crimson for coziness, burgundy for warmth and rosy tints for romance.

Through red we may also find release of our most passionate emotions. As such, it might be labeled the color of indiscretion with passion and sensuality the basis of a temporary fling. Red, therefore, can easily lose its beautiful positive vibes when emotional energies are focused only on physical gratification.

Artists, poets and writers have engaged color to express diverse emotions in their oeuvre. Dutch painter, Vincent Van Gogh looked hard at the world around him . In his night scenes, which the artist made between 1889 and 1890, he extended his depiction of night to the after dark entertainments of urban life, such as cafés and dance halls. In "The Night Café," for example, which he painted in 1888, Van Gogh observed the listless patrons of a bar underneath the harsh blazing glare of gas lamps at night. Commenting on Night Café Van Gogh said:

"I tried to express through red and green the terrible passions of humanity."

However, passion can be a good thing when it serves as an impetus to energize us forward and create new opportunities. Red can inspire heroism and courage and foster an optimistic outlook, while dark red indicates a high temper. Such a person is apt to be domineering and is quick to act, often without thinking things through. Faber Birren wrote:

"Red has more associations, more symbolism than any other color, signifying love and hate, patriotism and anarchy, sacrifice and cruelty, virtue and evil. A token of blood and fire, red is a color to which it is hard to be indifferent. It may be loved or feared, but it is seldom disregarded."

THE RED PERSONALITY: Red personalities are independent, often forward thinkers and can be pioneers in their field. They are ambitious, risk takers, passionate and have very strong leadership qualities. They are confidant and self-assured, a characteristic that color authority Audrey Kargere confirmed, "Exposure to the wrong colors can deplete, while the right color environment can recharge your batteries."On the nature of color this excerpt found in the Edgar Cayce readings says it succinctly:

"Color is the 'weather vane' that can serve as an indicator of a particular trend of mind or trend of desire."

Red empowers us with strength and a passion for living life to its fullest potential. Such a person is driven with ambition and determination to succeed. If you love red you are an extrovert, a take-charge person given to action. You're a born leader and a good administrator. Boss is your title at work and at home you rule the roost with an iron glove. That doesn't mean you're ruthless, because you praise others or admonish them, as the spirit moves. Red personalities may be quick to judge people but as Faber Birren wrote:

"Your temper swings more like a pendulum than like an axe."

Red personalities can be a whirlwind of activity, you live life in the fast lane and pack your agenda with thrilling new experiences and events. You're the first to see a new museum exhibition, get tickets for the world's most renowned orchestra, opera or ballet and you're on top of social happenings where you expect to be the center of attention.

It's never a dull moment in your presence because you're interesting and dynamic. Just being around you boosts an individual's outlook on life, which to you is meant to be a joyful experience. On a positive note, you will not tolerate any unpleasantness. Instead you look on the positive aspects of any situation taking up the mantra that life must go on despite disappointments or harsh realities.

However, the red personality isn't always popular. They can be self-centered and believe the universe revolves around their world. As they conceive and write their own life script, reds expect to get their own way, and other less powerful colors bend to their wishes. However, you do have deep sympathy within you and can take up a cause with the kind of passion that bleeds for humanity. You're a born activist and can be found in areas supporting political and personal causes.

RED HISTORY: Historically, painters created reds from natural pigments such as cinnabar and carmine. The ancient world also extracted red dyes from fruits, berries, barks and leaves. According to The Color Compendium:

"Reds presence in per-historic cave paintings make it one of the oldest colors used by man."

Other plant sources of red dyes included beetroot, cranberry and brazilwood. In addition to natural animal and plant sources, the classical world, since the third century, knew how to extract vermilion pigment by roasting cinnabar. Synthetic sources of red include alizarin, were first discovered in 1869 by the Germans Carl Graebe and Carl Liebermann.

Red comes from the old English "read," German "rot" and the Dutch "rood." It colors animal and plant names with vivid impressions. Think red fox, red oak, red maple, red dogwood, red currant, red delicious, and red cabbage.

RED CHAKRA: The Root Chakra (base of the spine) is located sat the seat of sexuality, the coccyx area. It is connected to the sexual, genital center, the gateway of passion, of birth and of survival. The pulsating swirl of red can seemingly dance down our body and engulf us with life giving energy. When the red energy comes to life, the Red Chakra is bright and clear and an individual's physical and sexual lives are healthy.

The Red Chakra controls all the solid parts of the spinal column, as well as the anus, rectum, colon, prostate gland plus the blood and building of the cells in the body, the bones, teeth and nails. In a balanced, healthy human being red activates vitality that says you're rooted in life and have the mental energy to fulfill its obligations.

For those individuals whose life may seem lackluster, or they feel fatigue, depression or melancholia they may overcome these tendencies with the life energizing red vibration in the food they eat, the clothing they wear or the environment in which they live. In the book, *The Seven Mansions of Color*, the author Alex Jones wrote:

"Red is also a great aid to those who are afraid of life and are inclined to turn their backs on the world or feel like escaping. The Red Ray helps to plant one's feet firmly on the earth. If a person is too spaced out---always living in the future---the red ray will help to root that person in the NOW."

The continuous flow of energy in your body depends on your daily activity. Thomas Gimbel advises:

"Do some 'gardening and get your hands dirty! This will help to 'ground' you and create a flow of energy through the emotional, mental, physical aspects of self."

MUSIC: The sound of red is C major and its chanted sound is U (ooh) and on the musical scale it is sung as Do. One only needs to listen to the red vibrations in stirring triumphant music to reeve up one's energy and revitalize their zest for life.

Hal A. Lingerman, a keen observer, in the *"Healing Energies of Music"* said: *"Musically our fiery nature likes power, surging sound, strong rhythms, and romantic, yet dynamic melodies, music of strength. I have observed that the fiery elements, often responds well to music of victory."*

Other testimonials to the power of red and music comes from French composer, Georges Bizet (1838-75) in a letter he wrote in 1859:

"Verdi has bursts of marvelous passion. His passion is brutal, it is true, but it is better to be impassioned in this way than not at all."

Lingerman's "Music of Fire" recommendations included the grand march from the opera Aida, by Italian composer, Giuseppe Verdi (1813-1901), as well as, the Overture and Prelude to Die Meistersinger, the masterpiece by German composer, Richard Wagner 1813-83).

Music lovers who are high wired, worried or in an emotional state may need to balance times of great energy and stress with periods of rest and reflection to foster a sense of peace and relaxation.

Again I reference Lingerman whose authoritative suggestions for this purpose include the Waltzes from Sleeping Beauty and Swan Lake by Russian composer, Pyotr Ilyich Tchaikovsky (1840-93).

COUNTERACT NEGATIVITY Music can also counteract negativity. In Dr. John Diamond's useful book, "Your Body Doesn't Lie," he mentions that the rock beat seriously hampers energy flow, and it distorts the senses, mental abilities and spiritual attunement.

He found that a young rock enthusiast who was having severe nervous problems responded strongly and positively to the soothing melodies of Czech composer, Antonin Dvorak's "Largo," one of the most famous pieces of classical music from his symphony No. 9. Under the influence of this music, the student was able to do his homework much more easily and creatively.

Positive red vibrations might also include melodies that paint a story with sound as a diversion from addictions to television and as a way to stimulate the imagination. Listening to musical pieces energize and awaken the mind. Fantasies and dreams come alive and the imagination soars to new heights of creativity.

For further uplifting vibrations listen to the wonderful orchestral interludes (known as the Four Sea Interludes) from the opera, Peter Grimes by English composer, Benjamin Britten (1913-76) as well as Appalachian Spring by American composer, Aaron Copeland (1900-90) to name a few.

The enormous range of all the beautiful and very rhythmical music selections can best serve as therapeutic medicine to increase one's creative sensibilities and invoke a vibrant and healthy outlook on life.

The practice of Music Therapy, however, is an identified therapeutic discipline administered by qualified practitioners. It is literally healing music prescribed to help you get better by the listening in a peaceful and quite environment.

EXERCISE OR YOGA: A highly energized individual obviously might consider ways to simmer down perhaps with gentle yoga as an exercise program. While we think of exercise as strengthening muscles and bones, yoga does just that plus a lot of things that vigorous exercise just doesn't do. Yoga works your spinal fluid and your international organs and systems-- cardiovascular, digestive and reproductive.

Another benefit of yoga is that a lot of toxins also get processed out of the body during the exercises. There are different disciplines in yoga practice so it is best to shop around to find the yoga class that best fits your needs. To make that assessment look for a yoga practice that offers a "free" introductory class.

Individuals who need to build up their body strength will find that gyms have a class for anyone who has lackluster energy or needs to pump up their stamina and improve their health. The exercise programs keep the endorphins flowing and soothe stressed minds.

There are other red themed activities to re-energize, such as, "white collar boxing" where clients slam a punching bag or compete in tug-of-war matches. From the sand volleyball court to the track these are places where you can speed up your day with renewed strength and energy. Power exercises can then connect you with your body's fullest potential.

Not interested in exercising like the pros?

Then try ethnic or traditional ballroom dancing. The fancy footwork will pump up cardio health and be fun at the same time.

FASHION: When wearing this color be prepared for excitement, good or bad. Red evokes strong images. Fiery red is Italian designer, Valentino's signature color which identifies with the gorgeous silk and precious lace gowns in his couture collection. He has always insisted on the magnetism of color.

"A gown in his signature red has always been synonymous with haute style," he has said, "When a woman arrives wearing one, everybody looks at her."

Then there are the legendary red designer gowns worn at the Oscars that invoke impressions of sexiness and ultra chic drama. Although red's seductive reputation translates to fashion as a hot, passionate color that says STOP, notice me, it can also fire up emotions and have angry consequences. Red is a bold, passionate color and, in its greatest force, it can alter the ecosystem of a room, but most significantly, it may perhaps change the fate of its wearer.

Color carries an emotional charge, it energizes feelings with passionate consequences. In recent years even scientists have admitted that individual responses to certain colors are charged with emotion.

Red, for instance, can conjure up such unpredictable rage that one needs to exercise caution as business attire in the workplace. Obviously, you would not wear a red hot suit for a job interview or to discuss a career promotion with your boss. It may get him so all fired up and agitated that you will have negative results. Chose soothing, serious navy blue instead.

Don't cancel out Red completely. To invoke positive vibrations, bold fire engine red is just what you want to wear for party and social occasions. Think of the powerful, come hither look of a strapless red taffeta cocktail dress, a curvy, hug-the-silhouette party dress or a striking red satin dinner suit. It says you're the kind of gal who isn't afraid to flaunt her femininity and sexuality.

FASHIONABLE APPAREL Red is versatile and is best for career apparel when subdued by the addition of black. A chic, fashionable jacket in a deep red shade has more wearable charm when paired with a pencil-slim black knee-length skirt. Add a crisp white blouse and the look is classic and says you're confident and professional.

The late Audrey Hepburn once said:

"There's a shade of red for every woman."

Traditional red tartans borrowed from the Scottish clans are always in vogue and a good classic investment. A tartan blazer as well as a pleated skirt or kilt can be worn year-after-year with stylish confidence, while bold red and black, lumberjack-inspired checks have rustic weekend wear sophistication. Such a fashionable lumberjack wool jacket coordinated with a black turtleneck sweater and sleek black leather pants arrests attention. When the same jacket is worn with denims it takes on a casual persona.

Accessories are usually an affordable addition to any classic outfit and red can give a color jolt to a basic black dress or black suit. Red accessories do not go unnoticed so punch up your wardrobe with a red leather handbag or a red python clutch. If you like to wear flats put red patent leather on your feet or wear fashionable red boots to declare your red independence. Every woman loves lipstick. Red always makes any face light up and rouged cheeks say you're vibrant and healthy.

A tip to joggers and gym enthusiasts. To pump up energy wear a red jogging suit or red patterned exercise gear which imparts vitality and energizes the activity. Don't laugh when you see red long johns in the underwear section of a Yankee catalog. Red's energy seemingly warms up the body, as does red pajamas and red socks worn on cold, chilly days.

HOME FURNISHINGS: Red is the power color. It is vibrant and energetic and is at home in most contemporary and classic decors. It's temperature, depending on its shade, can be warm or hot.

Red also symbolizes passion and romance. Renowned color authority, Jules Guerin, noted that red excites the mind. In a bedroom, for example, red can pulsate so passionately that it engulfs you and its vibration may unleash your reserve.

Although red can foster passion, too much red can be over stimulating , and a marital rift erupts. Then, too the use of ill-proportioned red in wallpaper as well as draperies may be the cause of headaches, nervousness and worse, a bad temper.

A more romantic and positive affect can be invoked with a red Toile de Jouy printed coverlet. Reminiscent of the 18th century French scenic pattern, the Toile's enchanting red and cream pastoral scenes give the décor more livable charm and a serene ambiance.

When it comes to love perhaps the poem by Scottish poet, Robert Burns says it all:

"Oh, my luv is like a red, red rose, That's newly sprung in June, Oh, my luv is like the melodie, that's sweetly played in June."

Red can also be the antidote to rejuvenate health. For instance, in a bedroom, where an invalid is recovering, the vibration of red can overcome depression and stimulate the will to live. Perhaps that is why some hospitals, which have now realized the value of color psychology, make red a dominant color in décor to stimulate recovery. The same red treatment can be applied at home. When you are sick with a cold or other ailment, try the red remedy and wrap yourself in a red blanket or wear a red robe.

EXOTIC RED Red can also be exotic and beckon with images of faraway places and treasures. Diana Vreeland, the doyenne of fashion, created original ethnic environments in the exotic red décor and the fashions she wore in her home. From 1937 to 1980s she was the arbiter of style, first as editor-writer for Harper's Bazaar and also as editor-in-chief of Vogue. Taking a cue from Vreeland, living room décor can be:

"As fascinating and as exotic as walls painted a deep red shade, such as maroon, with an under base of gold that twinkles as the sun light hits the wall. Keeping in step with the exotic, place a Moroccan rug on the floor and use giant throw pillows to sit on instead of chairs. As such, red can make a room look smaller and intimate. "

Red lacquer can work wonderfully to reflect a traditional Chinese décor by placing one or two red lacquered chairs among black lacquered furniture. Wear the finest red silk kimono robe and you may perhaps channel Vreeland's exotic style..

A red- red dining room should be avoided because it would evoke too much stimulation, pumping up emotions and also stimulating the appetite. As a result people eat in a hurry and they do not take the time to savor their food.

Red by choice is why fast food restaurants make it their signature color. They are more interested in stimulating appetites and moving customers in and out of their doors and making a fast profit.

However, more livable wall colors, such as wine-inspired shades of burgundy or merlot, can add drama to the dining environment, while the underlying red energy will keep the conversation lively. Bring balance into the décor with green plants, not just at Christmas time, but year round.

In areas where activity is the focus, the stimulating properties of red can pump up energy especially in a home gym environment. Red is also a vital asset in public gyms where strength, vitality and perseverance are paramount. Stairways and passageways could also use some kind of red to stimulate awareness and alert visitors to keep moving with a lively step.

PRODUCTS: Red packaging serves as a springboard for communicating a "sell" message to the consumer. Red never goes unnoticed. It can be so radiant and red-hot that it grabs your attention and says,'buy me.' That is why red is the captivating color choice for many shelf products. Why? Because red conveys strength and effectiveness and in soft drinks. Coke, for example, is the classic red brand.

The fragrance industry knows the power of red's passionate nature and numerous scents are bottled or packaged in red to entice women and men ,and thus pump up consumer spending. Cosmetic companies also take part in the red solution with red based lipsticks and matching blushes. However, other shades such as burgundy and wine give a bold berry sheen and a modern update to lipsticks.

The beauty industry is on a constant quest for innovative product development. New anti-redness products, for example, aim to cancel out red tones in skin and even rosacea with a yellow powder that is immediately and visibly effective.

Talk about getting notice in both fashion and technology, there's a new idea every day. The first red laptop computer designed for women caught on fast. Fashion designer Vivienne Tam and Hewlett-Packard teamed up and created the HP Mini Vivian Tam Edition, which is small lightweight and colorful. Its red and pink peony injected print exterior matched some of Tam's fashion clothing.

Kitchen products kick in the red drama with the brightest and hottest colors to warm up your home. Le Creuset's red oval casserole dish is so attractive you can use it as a serving dish right on the table. Red crystal goblets give new drama to dining room settings and red Lucite dining chairs add just enough of a red glow to keep company in an upbeat, happy mood.

Redesigning a home office may also need a jolt of bold red in office chairs to keep the work energy flowing, to which the product lines coordinate with red files. An extra long glass-topped dining or conference table with red hot X crossed legs keeps everyone focused and attuned to the red vibration.

There's warmth and novelty in modern furniture too. Take Danish designer Arne Jacobsens, his red egg chair is unique and comfortable, and seemingly says 'STOP,' notice me, take a seat.

Red, White and Blue products never fail to be patriotic. While exotic combinations of red, purple and hot yellow suggest Mexico or Latin America in pottery or colorful rugs.

EAT YOUR COLORS: Nature knows that in order to be healthy we need all the colors in the rainbow in our diet. Fruits and vegetables receive sunlight for growth and contain vital phytochemicals that are produced by the plant and help prevent disease. In order to become healthy and vigorous we assimilate color energies from plants into our diet through the process of digestion and metabolism.

Think of the delicious fruit possibilities to stimulate our appetite: red delicious apples, cherries, red currants, red plums, strawberries, watermelon, pomegranates, and vegetables: beets, red cabbage, red bell peppers, red-skinned potatoes, red kidney beans, red onions, radicchio and radishes.

Tomatoes are red because of a phytochemicals, called lycopene, which helps to lower the risk of cancer and heart disease. You can get your daily dose of antioxidants by eating berries and strawberries too.

Each vitamin vibrates to a color. If you are deficient in red you may need vitamin B. However, the highest and most potent concentration of health can be found in fresh food that is purchased "in season," the time of the year when it is grown and sold at the Farmer's Market.

TRIVIA: Red by its passionate nature is linked to fiery romances that fizz out with melting desire. Among the notorious romantic figures in history was Georgiana, the Duchess of Devonshire (1757-1806) who had affairs with the leading British politicians of the day, yet despite her sexual exploits she was loved by the multitudes.

Other women in historical sags were not so lucky. The 1850 novel, "The Scarlet Letter," is a classic example.

The novel by Nathaniel Hawthorne (1804-64) is set in the strict and unforgiving Puritan era in America. You may remember that the story is about Hester Prynne, who is accused of adultery. Considered so scandalous at the time she is made to wear a scarlet letter as a badge of shame because she bore a child out of wedlock. It is curious to note, however, that Georgina also had an illegitimate child, but she was not ostracized.

It is said that true, enduring love comes in a gentler package of rosy, pink hues. So remember when he gives you pink roses his intention is serious. Naivete about the language of flowers is essential when it comes to true love. For instance, when a Frenchman gives you a bouquet of red roses when you arrived in Paris; the color intent means passion, not an engaging romance.

Red also has a sinister and sexual connotation that is fiery and fearsome with names like Red Devil and Red Rage or the Red Flag of sexual passion. Think of the Blanche Dubois in Tennessee William's, *A Streetcar Named Desire* (1947). Dubois' lady-like attire deceptively conveys refinement, but when she privately wears a red kimono it invokes the truth beneath the robe, her nymphomania, which drives Stanley (Marlon Brando) wild.

Then there is the Red Light district, an area or district in a city where the looseness of morals is rampant, with red. When it comes to other fiery emotions we don't want to become suddenly furious and 'See Red.'Nor do we want to wind up being infuriated because we are 'In the Red,' which signifies being in debt or operating at a loss as noted in the red column in the ledger book (opposed to "in the black").

However, Red can sound out the alarm and we welcome the Red Alert. It will signal a state of an imminent danger, such as a natural disaster or enemy attack, and hope that the international philanthropic organization, the Red Cross will come to our rescue.

Red lights command attention and represent danger or a fire hazard and Red Traffic Lights signal us to STOP and wait for the green light to go. No time to wait? Take the Red-Eye and travel by airplane overnight to make a morning meeting . Then, too, you may develop the Red Eye, bloodshot eyes due to lack of sleep. However, after such a fast lane journey we don't want our adversaries to throw in a Red Herring, something intended to divert attention from the real problem or matter at hand.

However, we may catch someone Red Handed doing something illegal or committing a crime. Traveling by train? If you arrive at a railroad station look for a Red Cap, a baggage porter ready to serve, but he is often hard to find.

What is your political persuasion? In the political arena a Red State indicates one that is loyal to the Republican Party. (Blue for Democratic states).

In Russia there's the Red Square in Moscow, adjacent to the Kremlin, where St. Basil's cathedral with its fairy tale onion-shaped spires is no Disneyland, but a place where tourists visit to see the Red Army (the Soviet Army) military parades and Lenin's tomb. Red also represents communism or having a communist government such as: Red China, an informal name for the People's Republic of China, and the last of the Red-Hot-Reds, Fidel Castro's Cuba.

Let's hope that they'll pull out the Red Carpet when we become celebrities and arrive at a big ceremonial event, such as Oscar night. Red has inspired many lyrics and melodies. We can sing to the praises of "The Lady in Red," or sentimentalize over "Red Sails in the Sunset," and as our flag flies the Red, White and Blue we can salute and raise our voices with "The Star Spangled Banner."

Then let's Paint The Town Red with a Red Blooded strong and virile man, and celebrate boisterously on New Year's Eve by making the rounds at bars and nightclubs 'till the wee hours of the morning' when we have a Red Hangover. Then we may be Red Faced with over intoxication or embarrassment.

Avoid the red zone, football's danger zone near the goal line, but when racing take the Red line to reach top speed.

Red belongs to Christmas, St. Valentine's Day and the Fourth of July celebrations. If Fido could have his way with red he'd run for the Red Ribbon second prize award, similarly awarded in cat and horse shows.

Born in January your birthstone is Garnet. Those deep-red gemstones found in antique jewelry are classic and chic. A gift from nature, garnet is valued to protect and safeguard the wearer.

One thing is certain a red personality has a passion for life and everyone within your orbit is drawn to your energy and enthusiasm.

Chapter 13
THE DYNAMICS OF COLOR
Color Psychology

PINK
Romantic 'N Nice

Pink partakes of love and affection
A gentler side of the red connection

Infused with white a lovely tint
Pink roses evoke a romantic hint

Softer pink as a baby's bottom
Sweetness and innocence begotten

A sweet reputation, a feminine hue
Youthfulness and cuteness on review

'Pretty In Pink' the fashion cliche
Schiaparelli's Shocking Pink by day

Pompadour Pink inspired by a queen
Shell pink and salmon are so serene

Pink rooms tame tension and aggression
Relax, calms nerves, did I mention

Forget diets, Pink curbs appetite
Eat fresh cut watermelon to delight

Warm up friendships and true love
Pink comes in like a peaceful dove.

Chapter 13
THE DYNAMICS OF COLOR
Color Psychology

PINK
Romantic 'N Nice

What are little girls made of? 'Sugar 'n spice and everything nice, that's what like girls are made of' and they often admit to a preference for pink. Pink has a sweet reputation and is cupid's favorite color linking it to Valentine's Day.

A combination of red and the purity of white give each pink tint has its own personality. It may be pure and innocent but the amount infused by love is determined by how much red is present.

Vivid intense pink, which has a high degree of red, for example, radiates with vibrancy that makes one smile and see life through rose colored glasses. Red vibrations combine with white for keynotes of affection, caring, tenderness, friendship, harmony and universal love at its core. Lilly Pulitzer designer of the iconic colorful Lilly fashions once said:

"Anything is possible with sunshine and a little pink."

Long associated with youth and innocence pink symbolizes love, affection and a romantic spirit. In its purest interpretation it is linked to the maternal qualities of the Madonna and sentimentalization of motherhood. As such it invokes images of pink babies, angels, cherubs and putti.

However, pink does not have to be 'girlie' or cute. It can be sophisticated and chic, and is vital to the prettiness in women. Those who are fond of this tint are "in the pink" with loving thoughts and a rosy outlook on life. Pink is also the symbol of true romantic and consistent love. Red on the other hand is more inclined to be passionate and has a tendency to be associated with a less durable romantic intentions.

Faber Birren, the noted color psychologist and author wrote:

"While women are freely drawn to pink, men were too embarrassed even to mention it by name because of its association is with little girls and all things feminine."

However, nearly 60 years later, since this writing, pink has stepped up in the apparel industry. The pink divide has narrowed and men of a fashionable persuasion have embraced pink as their own, particularly in shirts and ties.

INFLUENCE: Like a kiss or a caress, pink can impart gentle responses and awaken romantic emotions. As such the pink personality craves affection and usually shuns the intensity of passion. Such a person seeks a sheltered and protected existence. The spoken word also has its relationship to pink. As noted by Glady Taber:

"Almost all words do have color and nothing is more pleasant than to utter a pink word and see someone's eyes light up and know it is a pink word for him or her too."

The pink hue connotes caring and favor by doting parents or relatives, a compassionate mentor or teacher. Think of children and pets, they, too, are the benefactors of such benevolence and senior citizens have grown to like pink as a recollection of childhood memories that evoke that "in the pink" happy feeling.

The devotion and caring qualities of pink and its link to maternal types call to mind the sentimental mother and child paintings by American artist, Mary Cassatt (1845-1926), one of the few women who exhibited with the Impressionists. The painter's renderings of intimate scenes of motherhood, such as "Woman Preparing to Wash Her Sleepy child (1880), is the quintessential image of unconditional love. The mother's embrace, the gaze of the child's intimate familiarity and trust speak to us of the innocent bliss and the wonderful security that a child feels in its mother's arms.

PERSONALITY: Love pink and you have a gracious, warm persona, much charm, gentle ways, endearing friendliness and a sensitivity towards others less fortunate than yourself. You're the constant optimist and you want life to be good for yourself and everyone else who basks in the rosy glow of your orbit. Your mantra is "I love others and I am loved."

Someone very fond of pink, for instance, desires to live in a protected environment where they can feel sheltered and happy. In the loving reflections of the innocent activities on a summer's day "William Merritt Chase (1849-1916) turned his attention to painting nostalgic images of American leisure and refinement bathed in pastels and summer white.

Color and personality has occupied the work of many scientific individuals including Dr. Max Luscher:

"The principle of the Luscher Color Test is that accurate psychological information about a person can be gained through his or her choices and rejections of colors."

A simple version of the test, using color cue cards, can be taken and interpreted quickly, and the layman can administer it to himself. However, this is not a parlor game. But it does help to find out how psychologically revealing color choices can be.

Nicole Amoroso wrote in "Circling Chase" for Avery Galleries, "In a portrait of Alice, titled "Tired" from about 1894, William Merritt Chase uses a rich palette of pinks and whites with accents of red. From Alice's tired expression and relaxed posture we can imagine that she has just comfortably collapsed into the large soft pillow with her pretty white frock billowing around her."

No less appealing in the pink phase are the landscape paintings Chase created of Shinnecock. in eastern Long Island, in which he communicated the joyful nature of his family's summer activities playing outdoors on the dunes.

Graceful and soft-spoken the words of a mother, sensitive to the needs of children, exudes tenderhearted pink comfort.

NAMING PINK: "A rose by any other name would smell as sweet," may be a quote from Shakespeare but there are other color names besides rose to consider. Think Miami Art Deco pink, Lilly Pulitzer pink, Flamingo pink that take inspiration from Florida where we find delicious concoctions of raspberry pink, strawberry pink and watermelon. Then, too, there are flower garden of pinks---Pink Roses, Pink Peonies, Persian Rose, Pink Carnations, Pink Hibiscus and Dusty Rose to name a few.

Did you know that in ancient times, pink was a color attributed to boys (not blue)? It was determined that the red undertone in pink represented courage and masculinity.

The change to pink for a girl is probably connected to the philosophy that pink is gentle and feminine. Delicate tints include pink jade, shell pink and pink roses, pink carnations and pink apple blossoms and baby pink.

HISTORY: The Maharajah of Jaipur knew a thing or two about the mesmerizing aspects of pink and constructed an entire fairy tale city with pink palaces and temples. In Persia, the ornate hanging gardens of Babylon had 300 varieties of roses. Throughout history roses have been a traditional symbol of love, treasured by kings and queens and revered by poets. In Shakespeare's play, Romeo and Juliet, Juliet recites:

"What's in a name? That which we call a rose by any other name would smell as sweet."

Countless other writers have alluded to the rose in prose and poetry. For example, the sentence "Rose is a rose is a rose is a rose" was written by Gertrude Stein as part of the 1913 poem, entitled, *"Sacred Emily."*

The phrase was parodied by countless other writers. For instance, Ernest Hemingway in his 1940 novel, *"For Whom the Bell Tolls,"* wrote, 'a rose is a rose is an onion.' Then there is famed fashion doyen Diana Vreeland's famous cliché:

"Pink is the navy blue of India," says it all about the vibrant palette of India's textiles and architectural wonders.

Stirring up a rich pink palette and exotic colors, Russian composer, Nikolai Rimsky-Korsakov (1844-1908), described his symphonic suite, "Sheherazade" as "a kaleidoscope of fairy tale images and designs of Oriental character."

ORIGINS: So where does pink come from? Red is the core element in creating pink. Think of red as the center to which different degrees of white are added to create pale and light derivative tints such as baby pink and juicy strawberry. Then, too, let's not forget Shocking Pink, Electric Pink or Pink Passion.

To create pink shades, gray or black may be added to red to create deeper tones like maroon or burgundy. Magenta, the deepest and most luxurious of the pink ladies was developed in 1859 as one of the first synthetic dyes. The Victorians loved this color and called it their own in fashionable attire as well as home décor. Magenta library walls, for instance, added a rich background for books on display.

The fashion world took to the magenta phase and one more so than others, was the renowned French Haute Couturier, Charles Frederick Worth. He fashioned magenta in crinoline silhouettes, that were draped with rich damask or taffeta textiles embroidered or adorned with silk tassels.

In the early days of America, pink was on the minds of the American colonists. They experimented with creating paint and one of the more interesting results was sour milk mixed with red pigment to make pastel pink. Paint companies today often identify with historical pinks such as the classic Williamsburg Rose or give names to a tint to associate with a celebrity or historical figure.

Pompadour Pink textiles printed with small pink flowers or bouquets on a white ground, for example, were a popular bedroom décor. The y may have been inspired by association with the celebrated beauty, the Marquise de Pompadour (1721-64) the mistress of Louis XV of France.

FASHION: Schiaparelli Pink also known as "Shocking Pink," is a color that comes out of the fashion world and is attributed to the celebrated Italian fashion designer Elsa Schiaparelli (1890-1973). Her witty and Surrealistic clothes and sizzling pink took the fashion world by storm in the 1920s and 1930s when the Surrealism art movement reacted against the formal-real world with fantasy and dreamy symbolism. As an avant garde fashion artist she commissioned some of the best artists of the period including Salvador Dali and Jean Cocteau to design fabrics and embroideries for her fashion collections.

FASHION TODAY: Popular American designer, Isaac Mizrahi, (b. 1961) also embraces the passion for pink. Like Schiaparelli, he has a sense of comedy in his work with vibrant combinations, such as, a two-tone cashmere and wool dress. The light bubblegum pink top and the red skirt makes it the perfect style for an evening of romance. His work and personality was made into a docufilm, *UnZipped*, which ran in movie theaters and still airs occasionally on television.

Every feminine woman wants one very special cocktail dress and Diane von Furstenberg, the queen of the wrap dress, serves up her version with a cherry pink taffeta that has all the earmarks of Latin flavor with ruffled asymmetric detail. Then, too, designer Tracy Reese's love affair with pink is evident in her office, where many of the walls are painted pink, and so is her desk.

Reese represented pink in almost every one of her dress collections. Sometimes it is azalea, sometimes shocking. Pink is a vibrant pick me up color that says you're confident, bold and like to be noticed.

However, looking "Pretty in Pink" may not be as easy to create for the "Desk Set," in the corporate world Why? Because wearing pink may convey the image of immaturity. However, a cherry pink jacket can be a dramatic and fashionable color to perk up an otherwise somber black suit with a pencil slim skirt.

Every working woman's wardrobe can do with a jolt of some pink. However, the tint of pink makes all the difference. Pink has its own vibrancy and seems to add a special glow to a woman's complexion. Depending upon a your skin tone, a confectionery pink blouse can make you look pretty as a princess, while deep fuchsia may give the competitive edge for darker skinned beauties.

Come summer be daring and wear a flirty pink sundress, or a pink polo shirt with yellow clam diggers and turn on the charm. You'll appear more lovable and approachable. On the plus scale, a preference for pink, the color of romance, suggests that you will attract many admirers.

When selecting lingerie or boudoir apparel nothing is more sweetly seductive than a lace trimmed pink silk camisole and matching tap pants.

HOME FURNISHINGS: Living in pink environment may not be for everyone, but monochromatic schemes can provide a special romantic glow in a living room, bedroom, powder room or even an entryway.

Soft tulip-pink walls can soothe frazzled nerves and set the stage for an oasis of personal calm in a career woman's bedroom. Caution is advised, however, because too much pink has such a calming effect it may diminish desire.

Yes, pink overload can zap your energy so pump up the décor with a fuchsia bed coverlet and toss on vivid yellow and blue pillows to bolster comfort and provide jolt of spirited color. If romance is on your mind put pink heart symbols in the bedroom décor and your companion will apparently become more lovable---so I have been told.

Alone by the telephone? On solitary nights wrap yourself in a cozy pink robe find a cozy nook and read a romantic novel.

Take inspiration from the decorators who abolish harsh bright lights in the living room. Instead give yourself and guests a special treat and use bubble-gum pink lampshades or pink light bulbs to soften the atmosphere and give a rosy glow to your complexion. Vibrant fuchsia pillows can make an otherwise monotone pink sofa look more inviting.

If you want to create a mind-body-and-spiritual retreat for quite contemplation, place cushy, velvety pink pillows on an armchair located in a sheltered corner of a room and slip into the silence of quiet contemplation.

Dorothy Draper, the most influential American interior designer in America at one time, also believed that color could elevate the spirit and cautioned against dreary surroundings saying:

"Theatrical colors combinations like Flamingo Pink and deep Green caused the pulse to quicken and the mind to lift."

She used vibrant, "splashy" colors in never-before-seen combinations, such as aubergine and pink, with a "splash" of chartreuse and a touch of turquoise blue.

At the mountain city of Petropolis in the State of Rio de Janeiro, Brazil at the luxury resort hotel, the "Cassino Hotel Quitandinha." her penchant for vivid and unexpected color was expressed with Hollywood drama. When it was opened in the 1940s it was the largest hotel casino in Latin America.

The lavish public areas, considered among the masterpieces of Dorothy Draper colorful oeuvre, include her signature "cabbage rose" chintz paired with bold stripes, her elaborate and ornate plaster designs and moldings and her black and white checkered floors with dramatic theatrical size furniture. Did I mention, the hotel's decorator was previously a Hollywood set designer. Interesting to note, Dorothy Draper's décor and furnishings for the legendary Cassino were restored in 2016 upgrading the Cassino with nostalgic glory.

Stateside, a bubble gum pink banquet in a cup cake restaurant in Hyannis, Massachuset'swith pink checkerboard décor conveys happy childhood imagery in a perfectly fairy tale world. No wonder children of all ages and adults flock to its charming ambiance to remind themselves to remember how sweet the world can be.

Privacy is a priority but even a powder room can be an inviting retreat, particularly when you add pretty pink bathroom hand towels and accessories. However, let nature's green balance come through with leafy hanging plants. If that is not available, you might tack an artificial green ivy garland around the bathroom window frame and vicariously bring nature into the environment.

For outdoor pleasures just sitting in a rose garden, where rose vines climb over the fence or burst out of a pot on the patio, is a visually intoxicating experience. In the contemplative setting the aroma of roses can do wonders to soothe and calm nerves and make you feel less tired. Similarly lush, sweet smelling peonies in a vase in any room, have a similar uplifting affect.

PRODUCTS: The relationship of Pink to femininity is clearly linked to the cosmetic and fragrance industry. Pink is a cheerful color. It reflects a healthy glow and makes most women look and feel gorgeous. However, when choosing a pink lipstick it is important to consider your skin tone. For example, women with pink tones should go for a blue-based pink lipstick, while women with yellow tones require a warmer, browner shade. If you're undecided, select a sheer rose gloss to highlight your lips.

Light-reflecting pink bronzes or powders give cheeks that lit--from-within glow and like the song suggests, "You're younger than springtime."

You can wear your heart on your fingernails with luscious, creamy-pink nail polish that is flattering for every skin tone. Just looking at pink nails can put a smile your face, seemingly tame tension and make you feel romantic all year long.

FRAGRANCE: Fragrance and the lovely rose has long been a poetic symbol of a woman's feminine prerogative. At a wedding ceremony, in ancient Persia, rose petals were scattered on top of the water in a canal, and under heat of the midday sun, aromatic rose oil was born. This legendary formula is perhaps the base recipe of modern day products from room fresheners, to candles and scented rose oil diffusors.

The flower power of pink through rose hips, the buds on the flower, are an abundant source of vitamin C. A daily dosage of powdered rose hips, for example, found at health food stores, is said to be a good source anti-inflammatory compounds and antioxidants.

Perfumers use the essence of essential oil, produced from roses grown in the famous flower producing area in Grasse, France as well as from Bulgaria's Kazanlik valley.

However, France with its association to Parisian chic, has a legendary reputation for producing rose-based perfumes. As a matter of fact, a French woman considers fragrance the most important accessory to her ensemble.

The romance with rose-based perfumes and 'eau de toilette' suggests ultra femininity. A favorite is Lancome's "Tresor." It makes a woman feel so feminine and alluring.

EAT YOUR COLORS: The more colors we eat the better is our overall health. Pink fleshy fruits like "raspberry" Morocco oranges have a rich orangey taste with a hint of berry. Melogolds are low acid and very sweet and taste like grapefruits. Then , of course, Watermelons are a taste pleaser any time of the year. Fill up with pink shakes made in the blender with strawberries and yogurt. Feeling love starved? Put pink icing (white icing with dash of red food coloring) on the cake and feel romantic any day of the week. For soothing comfort sip Rose Hip tea and feel anxiety and tension fade away.

CHAKRA: Pink is a secondary color and balances the Heart Chakra which correlates to the color green, a symbol of harmony, truth and unconditional love.

Pink keywords include love, passion, romance, compassion, happiness, softness, faithfulness, gentleness and kindness. In general pink gemstones like pink sapphire, rose quartz, pink opal and pink tourmaline are calming, soothing and relaxing. To promote positive energy in a room hang pink crystal garlands in windows to reflect light and bring in a loving aura from sunlight.

According to the Meaning of Colors by Sobriety Stones pink gemstones attract, increase or strengthen love, for yourself, or others. These are the kind of stones that smooth difficulties in both romantic and family relationships and assist with self esteem and self-love.

Wear pink gemstones or carry them with you when you want to present yourself as a peaceful, calm and loving person. Or place pink gemstones around your home or office to stimulate lovable interaction and beautiful responses. Write letters or notes and on pink stationery and you're sure to get a response.

TIBETAN SECRETS: You can increase your happiness potential and bring joyful renewal into your life just be spending a few minutes a day using easy-to-do Tibetan rituals.

Getting into a joyful, happy pink mood is as simple as getting off the couch and onto the mat and sitting straight in the classic yoga pose, just like the Tibetan monks do. And if the floor is not good for you, sit on a rigid chair. Start by breathing in and out, then chant the mantra, Ommmmmm several times. The OM vibrations stimulate feel-good hormones and gets you in the mood to focus and concentrate on meditation.

It is best to select a specific focus each time you meditate.

For best results, don't dwell on a myriad of personal subjects that might need improvement or balance, but clear your mind and choose just one concern. One day your thoughts and prayers may be for world peace, another day it may focus on family harmony, a third day organizations working with refugee children and so on.

There are so many concerns every day to pinpoint the focus of your meditation, but be sure to reserve some time to also think about love and the fulfillment of your heart's desire. To learn more about meditation. Access the Edgar Cayce website at www.edgarcayce.org. Then, too, learn about women praying around the world at www.womenprayerweb.com.

TRIVIA: Lovers beware of the message you are sending to your sweetheart, family or friends. Pink and Valentine's Day go hand in hand with pink roses, which elicit the emotions of pure, uncomplicated true love. Red roses may be a traditional choice for Valentine day as well, but be aware that their intent is different. Red roses represent passion and the possibly that this a temporary fling.

The sentimentalization about a rose's demise has been sentimentalized in many songs. Sir John Stevenson, (1761-1852) Irish composer of classical music collaborated with Irish poet Thomas Moore (1779-1852) in the Irish air written in 1805:

"Ti's the Last Rose of Summer left blooming alone, all her lovely companions are faded and gone."

Then to lift our spirits we'd like to toast with Pink Champagne (a sparkling white wine from the Champagne district of France) or imbibe a Cosmopolitan or a Pink Lady cocktail, but we don't want to see any Pink Elephants or receive a Pink Dismissal Slip at work.

Let's not acknowledge the Pink Ghetto, the 60s-70s catch all phrase for women's jobs in teaching, secretarial and nursing. Instead let's drink spiked Pink Tea at a wedding reception , and even though we may be Pink Collar workers lets lift our Pinkie Finger to Pink Ribbon recognition to stamp out AIDS.

'In the Pink' is a fashion phrase that connotes being fashionable. Wear a Pink Coat, inspired by fox hunt uniforms, and you're heading full gallop into fashion's favorite color.

In the month of November the venerable luxury house Hermes promoted "La Fete de la Couleur" (a party of color) and puts Paris in a sea of pink and orange to celebrate "International Children's Rights Day. The profits from Hermes' pink and orange scarf went to UNICEF.

"Think Pink!" and wear T-Shirts, jewelry, fashions or the iconic Pink Ribbon to support The Breast Cancer Research Foundation dedicated to preventing breast cancer and finding a cure.

Want a flattering glow to enhance your complexion? Simply plug in a pink tinted light bulb and the flattering glow will enhance your outlook with good reasons to expect compliments.

Scientific research has proven that violent prisoners become less aggressive after sitting in a bubble gum pink room. Then, too, hyperactive children likewise calm down in such a bubble gum pink environment.

Take a joyful break and turn back the clock and watch the classic 1960s film, "Funny Face," starring Audrey Hepburn, when fashion was like pink icing on the cake. The main feature, a Parisian fashion show, casts a rosy glow over the models. The scenes are enchanting and you'll be "Tickled Pink" to see Fred Astaire in the role of fashion photographer.

On a brighter note, see the world with a happy frame of mind, choose rose tinted glasses and welcome smiles as you pink your way cheerfully through the unexpected vicissitudes of life.

The power of pink can provide a cheery "can do" attitude and help you to remember the unabashed exuberance of the days filled with youthful enthusiasm.

Just look at the MGM film, "Legally Blonde," (2007) featuring Reese Witherspoon as Ellie Woods, and see how her "can do" pink persona and pink outfits make their debut when she goes to Harvard. Later as the young courtroom defender, she steals the scene with a triumphant pink exit.

Pink is luscious, pink is divine, it's romantic, it's shocking, it's perfectly pretty, it's compassionate, it's kind, it's considerate and sympathetic. No wonder it's the symbol of world peace!

"I try to apply colors like words that shape poems, like notes that shape music."

-Joan Miro

THE DYNAMICS OF COLOR
Brief RECAP: History and the Chakras

"The story of color is almost the story of civilization itself," said the famed color authority and scientist, Faber Birren.

(Faber Birren, COLOR, A Survey in Words and Pictures From Ancient to Modern Science, Citadel Press, div. of Lyle Stuart Inc., p. 11)

> *"All nature was colored and ancient man tried to emulate it. Color was identified with the sun, the stars, the rainbow, and looked upon with wonder and awe."*

Ancient civilizations of Atlantis, Lemuria, Nu and Alatia used color in therapeutic practices. So did the Egyptians, who were centuries ahead of the New Age thinkers. Legend has it that this enlightened society built temples where color healing took place. Sunlight shone through colored gems, such as rubies and sapphires, onto people seeking healing.

They also used pulverized gemstones on remedies for sickness--yellow beryl, for example, as a cure for jaundice. Just as women today covet the secrets of beauty and a youthful appearance when Egyptian women were seeking rejuvenation they entered The Temple Beautiful to bask in different colors for healing or rejuvenation. (Theo Gimbel, Healing With Color and Light, p. 21)

Doesn't this Egyptian wisdom remind you of the practitioners today who similarly use gemstones as a talisman to treat or improve health? Indeed, gem stone therapy has become very popular today by people seeking non-evasive alternative treatments to improve mind, body and spirit.

In ancient times color was a language. Every hue had definite significance. What early man chose for his garments, artifacts, or temples had less to do with modern conceptions of aesthetics than with a sort of occult functionalism. The very mysteries of life prescribed his palettes and he expected colors to protect him on earth, guide him safely to heaven, and symbolize the majesty of the universe. (Birren, p. 12-13.)

Nearly every race and civilization has had definite ideas about color. The American Indian had colors designated for a nether world,world, generally black, and an upper world of many colors.

"Red, yellow and black are masculine colors; white, blue, green are feminine." (Birren, p. 15)

Across the world in Tibet, the very moods of human beings have a mystical relationship to color. Light blue is celestial. Gods are white, goblins red, devils black. Similarly even in modern times, color continues to affect person's mood on either a positive or negative level. Furthermore, the ancient theory about the meaning of color has not changed: blue for sky, white for God, black for the devil. (Birren, p. 15)

Sanskrit teachings from Tibet, well over 2000 years ago, talk about "Chakras" energy centers in the body, which has its origins in the practice of Yoga. The word Chakra itself literally means "wheel" that generates energy. These power centers are represented by a specific color.

There are seven Chakras that correspond to the seven colors that lie in line with the spine. (Gimbel p. 64) The entire chakra system acts like a prism, which corresponds to the rainbow spectrum as follows:

Violet and the White Light Chakra (the crown) is the center of creative visualization and connects you to an infinite intelligence.

Indigo Chakra (the brow) is the spiritual "Third Eye" and promotes intuitive thinking and a higher lever of consciousness and inner wisdom.

The Blue Chakra (the throat, nose, ears, and mouth) is the center for creative expression and gives us the ability to communicate. In health matters blue battles throat ailments and in some cases even laryngitis.

According to Chakra practitioners the Chakra colors can be used to improve one's health or state of mind. For example, when you have a sore throat the Blue Chakra (the throat) is out of balance. Tying a blue scarf around your neck will help to soothe a sore throat and improve communication. (Guerin, Healing With Color)

The Green Chakra (the heart) is the color of balance and the center of harmony, understanding, compassion, the ability to give and receive unconditional love.

The Yellow Chakra (the solar plexus) symbolically relates to the stomach and digestion. Like the sun it descends into the nervous system and is the center of empowerment and happy feelings.

The earthier, Orange Chakra, (the spleen) rules the stomach area, the lower intestines, kidneys and adrenal glands. Orange promotes vitality and makes you feel youthful.

At the base of the spine, is the Red Chakra, (the root). It relates to our instincts of survival, the life force itself. It is the center of sexuality connected to passion. energy and the power to create. (Gimbel, p.64-65)

Through meditation you can activate a specific Chakra to improve well being, minimize stress, improve sleep, even cleanse our body of toxins.

Red, for instance, can be shocking and it can cause unexpected consequences. If your love life is lagging the color Red in bedroom décor can put passion back into romance and a white ceiling can signify pure bliss.

To the ancient Buddhists of India, man himself was a product of colors and the elements: the yellowness of earth, the blackness of water, the redness of fire, the greenness of wood and the whiteness of metal. (Birren, p. 18)

The Chinese have always diagnosed illness by reading the "color" of pluses, complexion, and the appearance of the body's tissues and organs. A red pulse indicates a numbness of heart, whereas a yellow pulse means the stomach is healthy. (Gimbel, p. 21)

No wonder, when we visit a Chinese doctor today one of the first things he or she might do is check our pulse, or look the tongue or nails to ascertain one's condition of health.

In Europe the science of Heraldry had its medieval roots in color symbolism. During the crusades the English soldier wore a white cross, the Frenchman a red cross and the Fleming soldier, a green one. Heraldry remains part of modern culture, particularly in England. (Birren, p. 48)

Color was also vital to the doctrine of the Four Humours. This system of medicine may have originated in Egypt and was common throughout Europe from the days of the ancient Greeks and Romans to the Renaissance. Each humour was assigned its own color and any imbalance in the humours was manifested in the color of the skin complexion, tongue, urine, and feces. (Gimbel, p. 21)

Liturgical stained glass windows in the churches throughout the world are a perfect example of how daylight illuminates colors with spiritual symbolism for meditation and prayer. In ancient times illiterate people relied on stained glass artwork to convey the stories of the Bible.

The French stained glass artisan family, Maumejean Freres, a prolific producer of liturgical windows, received the grand prix at the 1925 Paris Exposition Internationale des Arts Industriels Modernes for the work, "The Annunciation."

It is a stunning interpretation of glass caught in a web of leaded metal: red symbolized the life force, blue represented the celestial, the godly sphere and gold exalted the rays of wisdom through the illumination of the sun. (Guerin, 'Stain Glass Tapestries')

Color is an important part of culture. The scared and profane holidays of a modern world bear tribute to the convenience, if not the divinity, of the rainbow in glorifying things festive. Red belongs to Christmas, St. Valentine's Day, the Fourth of July. Green is for St. Patrick's Day. Yellow and purple represent Easter, and orange signifies the themes of Thanksgiving and Halloween.

Flowers also have symbolic meaning. A charming custom in celebration of Spring is the first of May's flower, the Muguet, the white Lily of the Valley. Another old fashioned custom, people wore a white carnation on Mother's day for the deceased, while the red carnation symbolized the living. (Birren, p. 50)

The language of flowers has much to be appreciated in its wisdom and symbolism. Red roses represented passionate love while pink roses indicated love blossoming on a more permanent level.

THE DYNAMICS OF COLOR
Art and Music Commentary

Color is sexy, color is volatile, color is persuasive, color draws us into its orbit of enticing characteristics that are at once pleasing or can engender a negative response.

Artists who use color as their primary creative element engender reaction to their creativity through the persuasive color messages underlying their work.

When we look at a painting that is pleasing to us, it is pleasing to us because color resonates in a very special personal way to each individual. No two reactions may be the same because the vibrations of the artist's color choices generate, in the eyes of the beholder, either a definite positive or negative response.

In gallery exhibitions you may hear expressions such as: "I love the artist's use of red." There may be other colors in the abstract painting but dominant red resonates because it is a power color that represents energy and excitement, something this viewer, may be seeking in their life.

In observations of another kind , viewers may be at once mesmerized by sun-drenched paintings that appear to be ablaze with illumination. The warm , sunlit yellow glow resonates with a feel good result that brightens an individual's outlook on life.

Artists are a unique breed. They search the inner circle of their soul to inspire their creativity. They work alone, their ideas grow out of the depths of their imagination. They are innovators, risk takers who create works that at the onset, "no one," is particularly demanding. Nonetheless, these artists, like solo fliers, they have the courage to take flight, with new ideas, and on the path of creativity they never stop until the work is done!

However, like any creative individual, they need to be inspired, but once they get inspired, they do not quit. They work around the clock to create something rare and beautiful, yes-- something never done before. Though the Great Master artists are classic, even the most abstract art is about something.

If it is a bold color study, it can jolt your emotions, wake you up and shake you up to react to the painting. A combination of pulsating colors just makes one feel happy gazing at the perky colors, while soft pastels soothe and calm down tempers.

Artists, for instance, who work in the primary colors, blue, yellow and red have specific color references in mind.

Blue is about heavenly thoughts and communication, dreamy yellow invokes happiness and a sunny disposition. Red, the power color channels the flame that ignites the heart with a will to live.

Color is a balancing act. The artist's choice of tints and shades resonate in a highly personal way to each individual. Images of men, women, children, animals ad places confront the gallery viewer with unexpected reactions to visual story telling. Each work chronicles a time, a place frozen in a frame that welcomes spectator appreciation.

Paintings in a gallery, for example, tell a variety of stories from different artists' perspective. One may shout loud and clear with colors that provoke you while others whisper soft and gentle with neutral tones.

All art in color and line communicate unforgettable color experiences through paint on canvas, ours to revere the unique gift of creativity. As the art experts say:

"Purchase art that you love, that pleases you, not because it is in vogue or you want to impress."

IF MUSIC BE THE SOURCE OF LOVE Musicians have views on art and music as two dynamic converging creative forms of expression. English musician, Yoni Higgsmith, for example, wrote:

"Art is how we decorate space; Music is how we decorate time."

Music is a very emotional experience. Like art, it too can crash into your sensitivities, and in some instances, even well up tears of compassion , remembrance of things held dear, lost love and yearning .

We react to music with very personal responses. With nostalgic memories. "Somewhere Over The Rainbow," from the Wizard of Oz, for example,conjures up childhood playfulness. Majestic symphonies with full orchestration, on the other side of the music scale, may lead us to reach heights of splendor bursting with colorful imagery

Memorable and unforgettable voices also contribute their colorful stories. For instance, the golden voice of a great opera singer, like the late Luciano Pavarotti, astounded audiences with his vocal dexterity and amazing sound. Like a great instrument, his singing seemed effortlessly powerful with incredible beauty and charged emotion. To experience the performance of such a singer is a gift, never to be repeated again. He was unique like a finely chiseled work of art.

Then, too, there are the popular ballad singers, story tellers of love, loss and even death. They connect us to a sentiment with lilting voices that bring audiences to their feet with unrivaled applause.

Concert singers seem to hold audience in the grip of their lyrics with personal interpretation that is a style of their own. Audiences may prefer such a singer for their singular ability to interpret a song that make their performance unique, special.

There is a unique magic about attending, hearing a live musical performance. Even the best recordings do not convey the majesty, the power and the passion, and the incredible excitement of the actual musical experience. You have to be there in the concert hall to fully realize the emotional and colorful impact that the music conveys to the listening audience.

The synergistic relationship between soloists, conductor and orchestra and the audience create a never to be repeated musicality that colors our life with a rainbow of emotions that elevate one to heightened levels of culture and civility.

The sound of colors is so definite that it would be hard to find anyone who would express bright yellow with base notes, or a dark lake with the treble.

-Wassily Kandinsky

THE DYNAMICS OF COLOR
Soul Mates Art and Music

"If you learn music, you will learn all there is to know."
                                                    -Edgar Cayce

"Art is not what we see, but what makes others see."
                                                    -Degas

"Light in nature creates the movement of color.
                                                    -Robert Delaunay

"Nature always wears the colors of the spirit."
                                                    -Ralph Waldo Emerson

"Music expresses that which cannot be put into words and that which cannot remain silent.
                                                    -Victor Hugo

"I found that I could say things with color and shape things I had no words for."   *-Georgia O'Keefe*

"Art washes away from the soul the dust of everyday life."   *-Pablo Picasso*

"I want to touch people with my art. I want them to say 'he feels deeply, he feels tenderly."
                                                    -Vincent Van Gogh

"The artist is nothing without the GIFT. But the gift is nothing without the WORK.   *-Emile Zola*

"When you sleep, all you do is dream, when you

stay awake, you make those dreams come true."

-David Aquino Sanchez

About the Cover Artist
DAVID AQUINO SANCHEZ

David Aquino Sanchez is a self-taught artist whose large repertoire of works in color identify with his diverse and multi--dimensional oeuvre.

Aquino Sanchez was born on September 20, 1980 in Bayaguana, Dominican Republic. As a child, he had a passion for drawing, but he spent his childhood and youth dedicated to sports and school.

It wasn't until the age of 26 when he already had mastery in drawing that he started to mix colors, and his works took on his individualistic style that features both modern and Surrealistic interpretations. He also discovered his ability to sculpt.

I chose Aquino Sanchez's painting SOUL MATES #1, for the cover of *The Dynamics of Color*, because his iconic art work so aptly represents the diverse subjects in the book in tandem with the dynamics of Aquino Sanchez's artistic expression.

Artist Statement

I am an open book with many blank pages that can only be filled by my art and the revelation of God, I am a story that doesn't have a specific point to end, I am a story not yet told that will echo into eternity.

I search in my brushes, canvas, and colors for the general meaning of creation, and I have been able to find myself in my search through art. The wood and marble are elements, that while I sculpt, I feel I can step into direct contact with nature.

Sometimes I think that it is my sculptures that give form to my thoughts and not me to them. I use the camera lens to capture the beauty of my environment. Through photography, I confirm what has already been seen by the Quasi-divine eye given by God to transcend the vision to something permanent and not erasable.

That is why my ideas and thoughts always go hand in hand with my visions. My creations and ideas flow from my subconscious. Through my art, I intend to create a universe of colors where what is infinite does not exist! I think an artist is born an artist and dies an artist.

Contact the artist: El.Artista.Aquino@gmail.com

COLOR TERMINOLOGY

Achromatic: Colorless, lacking in color

Advancing Colors: Colors giving the illusion of nearness in the spectrum. Red-orange is warm, therefore, advancing and stimulating.

Aniline Colors: Synthetic, produced from coal-tar products.

Brilliant: A high degree of brightness.

Chrome: An intense undiluted color, free from white or gray.

Colors: The hues, tints and shades produced through the rejection of light by the retina of the eye.

Complementary Colors: On the color wheel. Two opposite hues which provide completeness to each other.

Cool Colors: Seemingly control temperature in a room like blue.

Dominant Color: A key color that dominates, stands out.

Fashion Colors: The color names created by fashion color consultants.

Hue: Synonyous with Color. The term used to distinguish on color from another.

Intense: Vivid, deeply immersive, full colors.

Monochromatic: The gradation of the shades of one color creating an ombre effect.

Organic Colors: Popular today. Pigments of animal and vegetable dyestuffs.

Pale Color: Very light value of a color.

Palette: Artists' pigments on a palette board.

Pigment: From the Latin term "Pigmentum" meaning paint.

Secondary Colors: Two primary colors combined in equal proportion.

Spectrum: Primary colors caused by a beam of light broken up. Sir Isaac Newton's theory. The wave length of each color is separated, forming a series of hues—red, orange, yellow, green, blue and violet. Nature's rainbow contains these colors.

Sensation: The perception of color by the mind after the initial reception by the eyes.

Tint: A pale or light value of a color.

Tone: A hue used to reduce or subdue the intensity of a color.

Vibration: Everything in the universe has a specific rate of vibration.

Warm Colors: Seemingly warm up a room. Colors in which red or yellow predominate. These colors psychologically are associated with heat, the sun and fire

Wave Length: The distances between the vibrations of light that produce visible colors Red-orange procures the longest wave length, while violet has the shortest.

"We are all broken, that's how the light gets in."

-Ernest Hemingway

WHO'S WHO IN THE BOOK

Joseph Albers: German artist and educator (1888-1976). His book, *Interaction of Color* presented the theory that colors were governed by an internal and deceptive logic. The work has been re-published and is now available as a cell phone app.

Dr. Edward J. Babbit: (1816-unknown) Renowned educator, instructor, lecturer, research writer and visionary pioneer. Author of *Principles of Light, Tone and Color*.

Faber Birren: American author and industrial color consultant. (1900-1988). He advised clients on the psychological effects of color on safety, employee morale productivity and sales. Wrote 40 books 250 articles.

William Blake: British poet and painter (1757-1827). Both his poems and his paintings have a mystical, visionary quality. His first volumes of poetry Songs of Innocence.

Edgar Cayce: (1877-1945) Famous prophet, psychic counselor and healer. Recognized internationally. Best known in his field and books on color including "Color and the Edgar Cayce Readings" by Roger Lewis.

Theo Gimbel: Color theorist, counselor and international speaker (1820-2014) . A respected figure on the subject of color and its influence on health and well being. His first book book, Healing Through Color, then wrote Form, Sound, Colour and Healing.

Jules Guerin: American-born French Artist (1886-1946). Frequent collaborator with architects. Director of color and murals for for numerous great buildings including the Lincoln Memorial Building, Washington, DC and Federal Reserve Bank in San Francisco, California.

Audrey Kargere: (1910- unkown) Color authority, lecturer, educator. Author of the book, Color and Personality, reprinted numerous times. PhD Studied at the Sorbonne, Paris, France.

Dr. Max Luscher (1923-2017) Swiss psychotherapist. He invented The Luscher Color Test, which has been translated into 30 languages. *The book translated and edited by Ian Scott.*

Ernest J. Stevens, M. SC, PhD, MA (1864-1944) Author of Vibrations, Their Light, Tones and Color Published by Health Research Books. Maintained Light & Color Research Studios in San Francisco. Wrote the poem "Rainbow" in 1938.

BIBLIOGRAPHY

Augustine Hope and Margaret Walsh, *The Color Compendium*, Van Nostrand Reinhold, New York, 1990

Babbitt, Edwin D. *The Principles of Light and Color*, New Hyde Park, N.Y.: University Books Inc., 1967

Birren, Faber, *Color Dimensions, Creating new Principles of Color Harmony*, Chicago, Crimson Press, 1934
_____Color, A Survey in Words and Pictures, The Citadel Press, Secaucus, N.J., 1963
_____*Color Psychology and Color Therapy*, The Citadel Press, Secaucus, N.J., 1950, 1961

Burrows, John, Classical music, Dorling Kindesley Ltd, New York, NY., 2004

Cayce, Edgar, *Auras*, A.R.E. Press, Virginia Beach, Virginia 1945

Clark, Linda, The Ancient Art of Color Therapy, The Devin-Adair Company, Old Greenwich, CT., 1975

Finlay, Victoria, Color, A Natural History of the Palette, Random House Publishing Group , a division of Random House Inc., New York, N.Y., 2004

Garfield, Laeh Maggie, *Sound Medicine*, Celestial Arts, Berkeley, CA.Inc, 1987

Gass, William, On Being Blue, A Philosophical Inquiry, 4th printing, David R. Codine, Publisher, Boston, MA., 1978

Gimbel, Theo, *Healing Through Color and Light*, Simon & Schuster, Inc., Gaia Books Ltd., London, England, 1994
_____Form, Sound, Colour and Healing, The C.W. Daniel Company LTD , Essex, England, 1987

Guerin, Polly, *The Story of Color*, Fairchild Books & Visuals, New York, N.Y., 1987.
_____Sacred Spaces, Open Door Oct-Dec publication, Volume XXIV, Issue 4, A.R.E New York Center, 2017.

Heline, Corinne, *Color and Music in the New Age*, New Age Press, Inc., Oceanside, CA. 1964

Jones, Alex, *Seven Mansions of Color*, DeVorss & Company, Marina de Rey, CA., 1982

Kandinsky, Wassily, *The Art of Spiritual Harmony*, Houghton Mifflin Co., Boston, 1914

Kargere, Audrey, *Color and Personality*, Philosophical Library Inc., New York, N.Y., 1949, reprinted 1990.

Kirkpatrick, Sidney, Nancy, Managing Editors, Venture Inward quarterly magazine, A.R.E. Press, Association for Research and Enlightenment , Virginia Beach, VA., 2017

Lacy, Marie Louise, *Know Yourself Through Color*, The Aquarian Press, an imprint of Harper Collins Publishers, San Francisco, CA., 1989

Lewis Roger, Color and the Edgar Cayce Readings, A.R.E. Press Virginia Beach, Va., 1987

Luscher, Dr. Max, *The Luscher Color Test*, translated and edited by Ian Scott, Random House, Inc., New York, N.Y., 1943

Mayer, Gladys, *Colour and Healing*, New Knowledge Books, Sussex England, 1960

Wagner, Carlton, The Wagner Color Report, Wagner Institute for Color Research, Santa Barbara, California, 1988

Wood, Berry, *The Healing Power of Colour*, Destiny Books, Rochester, Vermont, 1984

ASSOCIATIONS

Association for Research and Enlightenment of New York , (A.R.E.) the Edgar Cayce Center 153 West 27th Street, Suite #702 , New York, N.Y. 10001. 212 691-7600, edgarcaycenyc.org.

The Association for Research and Enlightenment Inc., (A.R.E.) 215 67th Street, Virginia Beach, VA 23451-2061. 800.333.4499. EdgarCayce.org.

EDGAR CAYCE (1877-1945) founded the non-profit Association for Research and Enlightenment (A.R.E) in 1931 to explore spirituality, holistic health, intuition, dream interpretation, psychic development, reincarnation, and ancient mysteries---all subjects that frequently came up in the more than 14,000 documented psychic readings by Cayce.

The A.R.E. Provides individuals from all walks of life and a variety of religious backgrounds with tools to help them to change their lives for the better physically, mentally and spiritually.

For in-depth information on the life of Edgar Cayce contact EdgarCayce.org.

RESOURCES

Dr. Scott J. Keller, Caycean Chiropractor, drscottkeller.com

Tattfoo Tan, Nature Matching System (NMS) tattfoo.com

THANK YOU

Thank you for choosing my book, **Dynamics of Color** to enhance your understanding of how color is a dynamic force in every aspect of your life.

Polly Guerin

Polly

Comments are always welcome. Please email pollytalknyc@gmail.com

Visit Polly's homepage www.pollytalk.com and click on the links in the left hand column to her Blogs on visionary men, women determined to succeed, poetry from the heart and her long running Monday column on cultural and social events on the Internet: www.pollytalkfromnewyork.blogspot.com

Made in the USA
Columbia, SC
14 March 2018